M000285377

101 Things®
To Do With
a Pickle

101 Things To Do With a Pickle

BY
ELIZA CROSS

GIBBS SMITH
TO ENRICH AND INSPIRE HUMANKIND

24 23 22 21 20   5 4 3 2 1

Text © 2014 Eliza Cross

101 Things is a registered trademark of Gibbs Smith, Publisher
and Stephanie Ashcraft.

All rights reserved. No part of this book may be reproduced by
any means whatsoever without written permission from the
publisher, except brief portions quoted for purpose of review.

Published by
Gibbs Smith
P.O. Box 667
Layton, Utah 84041

1.800.835.4993 orders
www.gibbs-smith.com

Printed and bound in Korea
Gibbs Smith books are printed on either recycled, 100% post-consumer
waste, FSC-certified papers or on paper produced from sustainable PEFC-
certified forest/controlled wood source. Learn more at www.pefc.org.

Library of Congress Control Number:2019948129

ISBN 978-1-4236-54681

For Laura Fallbach, with whom I've
gotten into more than a few pickles.

www.gibbs-smith.com

CONTENTS

Pickle Kidney Bean Salad 64 • Pickle Pasta Salad 65 • Cuban Chicken Salad 66 • Shrimpickle Salad 67 • Chilled Pickles and Tomatoes with Warm Bearnaise Sauce 68 • Macaroni, Pickle, and Ham Salad 69 • Danish Cobb Salad 70 • Deluxe Cheeseburger Salad 71 • Triple Green Salad 72

Sandwiches

Cheesy Pickle Panini with Roast Beef 74 • Classic Dagwood Sandwich 75 • New Orleans Pickle Muffaletta 76 • Pickle and Tuna Melt 77 • Zesty Reubens 78 • Dill Picklicious Turkey Wraps 79 • Scandinavian Open-Face Sandwich 80 • Fried-Pickle Burgers 81 • Bratwurst with Pickles, Bacon, and Onions 82 • Pickle and Ham Salad Rolls 83 • Pickle Pigs in Blankets 84 • Pork 'n' Pickle Burgers 85 • Pickle Sliders 86 • Grilled Ham, Cheese, and Pickle Sandwich 87 • Stuffed Turkey Burgers 88 • Barbecued Pickle Porkwiches 89

Side Dishes & Breads

Roast Pickle Potatoes 92 • Dilly Deviled Eggs 93 • Zippy Succotash 94 • Sweet and Sour Vegetables 95 • Dilly Green Beans 96 • Dill Pickle Bread 97 • Pickle Biscuits 98 • Cheesy Pickle and Artichoke Muffins 99

Dinners

Pickle Cheeseburger Pie 102 • Grilled Pickle Steaks 103 • Dill Pickle Meatloaf 104 • Cuban Pork Tenderloin 105 • BBQ Pickle Pizza 106 • Creamy Dill Pickle Chicken 107 • Salmon Filets with Dill Pickle Sauce 108 • Beef Pickle Stroganoff 109 • German Rouladen Rolls 110 • Marinated Pickle Chicken 111 • Slow Cooker Pickle Pork 112 • Ham and Cheese Pickle Pockets 113 • Sausage Calzones 114 • Pickle Fondue 115 • Farmer's Casserole 116 • Chesapeake Casserole 117

Desserts

Pickle Cupcakes with Lemon-Cream Cheese Frosting 120 • Sweet Pickle Ice Cream 122 • Sweet Pickle Pie 123 • Big Daddy Pickle Cake 124

HELPFUL HINTS

1. When making your own pickles, use ripe pickling cucumbers, which are shorter and chunkier than regular eating cucumbers. Choose dark green, firm cucumbers with spiny bumps on the surface. Cucumbers with yellow or white spots may be overripe, resulting in mushy pickles. Make sure cucumbers have not been coated in wax, as the pickling brine cannot penetrate it.

2. Scrub fresh cucumbers well, and remove and discard a $\frac{1}{4}$-inch slice from the blossom end. Blossoms may contain an enzyme that causes pickles to soften.

3. Quick pickles, also known as refrigerator pickles, should generally be eaten within a month.

4. Brined pickles use a fermenting process, and often an additional acid like vinegar, to preserve the pickles over an extended period of time. Quality is best if eaten within 6 months.

5. When making your own brined pickles, hard water may interfere with the formation of acid and prevent pickles from curing properly. Use distilled or soft water for best results.

6. Use non-iodized canning or pickling salt for fermented pickles, not table salt. Iodized table salt may impede the fermenting process.

7. Use a high-grade cider or white distilled vinegar of 5 percent acidity, which is the vinegar commonly sold in most stores. Do not use homemade vinegars or vinegars of unknown acidity.

8. For best flavor, always use fresh spices when making pickles.

9. The pot used for the brine should be stainless steel, anodized aluminum, glass, or enamelware that is free from chips.

10. When preparing brined pickles, the cucumbers must be kept submerged in the brine, usually by putting a weight like a plate on top of the pickles.

11. Never alter the ingredients or proportions in the brine recipe.

12. Glass canning jars should be free of chips or cracks. Do not reuse jars and lids from commercially-canned foods. For best results, use canning jars with two-piece lids that form a vacuum seal when processed.

13. Do not use copper, brass, low grade aluminum, galvanized or iron utensils when making homemade pickles. These metals can react with acids or salts and cause undesirable flavors and colors in the pickles.

14. To sterilize jars before filling with pickles, wash jars and lids with hot, soapy water. Rinse well and arrange jars and lids open sides up, without touching, on a tray. Boil the jars and lids in a large saucepan, covered with water, for 15 minutes.

15. Use tongs when removing jars from boiling water. Be sure tongs are sterilized by dipping the ends in boiling water for a few minutes.

16. After filling the jars to the recommended level, wipe the rims with a damp paper towel. Tap the jars to remove any air bubbles before screwing on the caps.

17. Process the sealed jars by placing them in a large pot of boiling water for the recommended time. (Check with your county extension agent for the recommended time for your area.) The boiling water in the pot should completely cover the top of the jars. After placing jars in the boiling water, always wait until the water returns to a full boil before counting the time required for the processing.

18. Store refrigerator pickles in the refrigerator. Fermented pickles should be labeled, dated, and stored in a cool, dark place.

19. Discard any home-preserved pickles with an off odor or color.

HOMEMADE PICKLES, RELISHES & SAUCES

CRISP REFRIGERATOR PICKLES

2 cups	**sugar**
1 cup	**distilled white vinegar**
1 tablespoon	**salt**
6 cups	**sliced pickling cucumbers**
1 cup	**sliced onion**
1 cup	**sliced green bell pepper**

Combine the sugar, vinegar, and salt in a medium saucepan. Over medium heat, bring the mixture to a boil and cook, stirring occasionally, until the sugar has dissolved, about 10 minutes.

Combine the cucumbers, onion, and bell pepper in a large bowl. Pour the vinegar mixture over the vegetables. Transfer to sterile containers, seal, and store in the refrigerator; use within 1 month. Makes 10 cups.

QUICK MICROWAVE BREAD-AND-BUTTER PICKLES

1	**large pickling cucumber,** thinly sliced
1	**small onion,** thinly sliced
1/2 cup	**sugar**
1/2 cup	**distilled white vinegar**
1 clove	**garlic,** peeled and crushed
1 teaspoon	**salt**
1/2 teaspoon	**mustard seeds**
1/4 teaspoon	**celery seeds**

In a medium microwave-safe bowl, combine cucumber, onion, sugar, vinegar, garlic, salt, mustard seeds, and celery seeds. Microwave on high 7–8 minutes, stirring twice, until cucumbers are tender and onion is translucent. Transfer to sterile containers, seal, and store in the refrigerator; use within 1 month. Makes about 2 1/2 cups.

ICEBOX DILL PICKLE SPEARS

4 cups	**water**
½ cup	**distilled white vinegar**
4 tablespoons	**kosher salt**
4 cloves	**garlic,** peeled and minced
I bunch	**fresh dill weed**
6	**medium pickling cucumbers,** cut into spears

In a medium saucepan over medium-high heat, combine the water, vinegar, and salt, and bring to a boil. Sterilize 4 (I-pint) jars, lids, and rings, and keep them hot.

Divide the minced garlic between the jars and add several sprigs of dill to each. Arrange the cucumber spears in the jars, packing in as many as you can without forcing.

Fill the jars with the hot vinegar mixture, leaving ¼-inch headspace at the top of the jars. Tap the jars to remove any air bubbles, screw on the caps, and refrigerate for at least 2 days before eating. Store in refrigerator and use within I month. Makes 4 (I-pint) jars.

SPICY REFRIGERATOR PICKLES

12 (3–4-inch)	**pickling cucumbers,** cut into spears
2 cups	**water**
1 3/4 cups	**distilled white vinegar**
1 1/2 cups	**chopped fresh dill weed**
1/4 cup	**sugar**
8 cloves	**garlic,** peeled and chopped
1 1/2 tablespoons	**coarse salt**
1 tablespoon	**pickling spice**
1 1/2 teaspoons	**dill seed**
1/2 teaspoon	**red pepper flakes** (or up to 1 teaspoon for very spicy pickles)
3 sprigs	**fresh dill weed**

In a large bowl, combine the cucumbers, water, vinegar, dill, sugar, garlic, salt, pickling spice, dill seed, and red pepper flakes. Stir until the sugar and salt dissolve, and let stand at room temperature for 2 hours.

Sterilize 3 (1 1/2-pint) wide-mouth jars, lids, and rings, and keep them hot. Use a slotted spoon to remove the cucumbers from the liquid and divide among the jars, arranging the spears upright until just full. Ladle in the liquid from the bowl to cover. Place a sprig of fresh dill into each jar, and seal with lids. Refrigerate for 10 days before eating. Store in refrigerator and use within 1 month. Makes 3 (1 1/2-pint) jars.

OLD-FASHIONED GARLIC PICKLES

8 pounds	**small pickling cucumbers,** 2–2$\frac{1}{2}$ inches long
3 tablespoons	**pickling spice**
4 cups	**water**
4 cups	**distilled white vinegar**
$\frac{3}{4}$ cup	**sugar**
$\frac{1}{2}$ cup	**pickling salt**
7	**fresh dill flower heads or sprigs**
7 cloves	**garlic,** peeled

Wash and place cucumbers in a large pot, cover with ice cubes, and let sit for 2 hours. Drain and pat dry. Wrap the pickling spice in a small square of cheesecloth and tie securely with a piece of kitchen string. Combine the water, vinegar, sugar, pickling salt, and cheesecloth-wrapped pickling spice into a large saucepan. Bring to boil over medium-high heat; reduce heat and simmer for 15 minutes.

Sterilize 7 (1-quart) jars and lids in boiling water. Pack the cucumbers into the hot, sterilized jars, filling to within $\frac{1}{2}$ inch of the top. Place 1 dill head or sprig and 1 clove garlic in each jar. Pour the hot pickling liquid into the jars, filling to within $\frac{1}{4}$ inch of the rim and discard the spices. Wipe the rims of the jars with a damp paper towel.

Tap the jars to remove any air bubbles, screw on the caps, and process them in a boiling-water canner for 10 minutes, or the time recommended for your area by your county extension agent. Cool the jars and press the top of each lid with a finger, ensuring the seal is tight and that the lid does not move up or down at all. (If any jars have not sealed properly, refrigerate them, and eat the pickles within 2 weeks.) Store sealed jars in a cool, dark place for at least 1 week before opening. Makes 7 (1-quart) jars.

SWEET-AND-SOUR MUSTARD PICKLES

7 1/3 cups	**water,** divided
3/4 cup	**pickling salt**
3 1/2 pounds	**small pickling cucumbers,** 2–2 1/2 inches long
4 cups	**distilled white vinegar**
2 cups	**sugar**
4 teaspoons	**mustard seeds**
3/4 teaspoon	**ground turmeric**
3/4 teaspoon	**celery seeds**

In a large saucepan, heat 6 cups of the water to boiling and add the pickling salt. Stir until dissolved. Place the cucumbers in a large crock or glass container and pour the salt mixture over them. Let stand until cool; drain and discard the liquid.

Combine the remaining 1 1/3 cups water, vinegar, sugar, mustard seeds, turmeric, and celery seeds in a large saucepan over high heat and bring to a boil. Pour liquid over cucumbers; let stand, covered, for 24 hours.

Sterilize 5 (1-quart) jars, lids, and rings, and keep them hot. Pack the cucumbers into the jars, leaving 1/2-inch headspace at the top of the jars. Fill the jars with the vinegar mixture, leaving 1/4-inch headspace at the top of the jars. Wipe the rims of the jars with a damp paper towel. Tap the jars to remove any air bubbles, screw on the caps, and process them in a boiling-water canner for 10 minutes, or the time recommended for your area by your county extension agent. Cool the jars and press the top of each lid with a finger, ensuring the seal is tight and that the lid does not move up or down at all. (If any jars have not sealed properly, refrigerate them, and eat the pickles within 2 weeks.) Store the sealed jars in a cool, dark place for at least 1 week before opening. Makes 5 (1-quart) jars.

GRANDMA'S 7-DAY PICKLES

1 1/2 gallons	**water,** divided
1 cup	**pickling salt**
6 pounds	**pickling cucumbers,** cut into 1/4-inch slices
1 tablespoon	**powdered alum**
1 tablespoon	**powdered ginger**
1 quart	**white distilled vinegar**
6 cups	**sugar**
1 tablespoon	**celery seeds**
1 tablespoon	**ground cloves**
1 teaspoon	**cinnamon**

Combine 1/2 gallon of the water and the salt in a large pot, and bring to a boil over medium-high heat. Place the sliced cucumbers in a large crock or glass container, and pour the hot salt water over them. Put a plate on top of the cucumbers to keep them submerged. Cover with a clean dishcloth and let stand at room temperature, undisturbed, for 4 days. On the fifth day, drain the cucumbers, rinse them well with cold water and drain again. Combine 1/2 gallon of the water and the alum in a large pot, and bring it to a boil over medium-high heat. Return the cucumbers to the large crock or glass container, and pour the hot solution over them. Put a plate on top of the cucumbers to keep them submerged, cover with a clean dishcloth, and let stand at room temperature, undisturbed, for 1 day.

On the sixth day, drain the cucumbers, rinse them well with cold water, and drain again. Combine the remaining water and the ginger in a large pot, and bring it to a boil over medium-high heat. Return the cucumbers to the large crock or glass container, and pour the hot solution over them. Put a plate on top of the cucumbers to keep them submerged, cover with a clean dishcloth and let stand at room temperature, undisturbed, for 1 day.

On the seventh day, sterilize 5 (1-quart) jars, lids, and rings, and keep them hot. Drain the cucumbers well. Combine the vinegar, sugar, celery seeds, cloves, and cinnamon in a large pot, and bring it to a boil over medium-high heat. Add the cucumbers and bring to a boil again.

Fill the jars with the hot mixture, leaving $1/4$-inch headspace at the top of the jars. Wipe the rims of the jars with a damp paper towel. Tap the jars to remove any air bubbles, screw on the caps, and process them for 10 minutes in a boiling-water canner, or the time recommended for your area by your county extension agent. Cool the jars and press the top of each lid with a finger, ensuring the seal is tight and that the lid does not move up or down at all. (If any jars have not sealed properly, refrigerate them, and eat the pickles within 2 weeks.) Store the sealed jars in a cool, dark place for 3–4 weeks before opening. Makes 5 (1-quart) jars.

BABY GHERKINS

2 pounds	**small pickling cucumbers,** 1 1/2–2 inches long
1/2 cup	**pickling salt,** divided
2 cups	**distilled white vinegar**
2 cups	**water**
1 tablespoon	**finely chopped onion**
1 clove	**garlic,** peeled and halved
1 teaspoon	**chopped fresh dill weed**
1 1/2 teaspoons	**black peppercorns**
2	**cloves**
2	**bay leaves**

In a large bowl, combine the cucumbers with 1/4 cup plus 2 tablespoons of the salt. Arrange the cucumbers on paper towels in a single layer to drain for 90 minutes. Rinse the cucumbers thoroughly and drain.

In a medium saucepan over medium-high heat, combine the vinegar, water, and remaining salt, and bring to a boil. Sterilize 2 (1-pint) jars, lids, and rings, and keep them hot. Divide the onion, garlic, dill, peppercorns, cloves, and bay leaves evenly between the jars. Pack the cucumbers into the jars, leaving 1/2-inch headspace from the top of the jars. Fill the jars with the hot vinegar mixture, leaving 1/4-inch headspace at the top of the jars. Wipe the rims of the jars with a damp paper towel. Tap the jars to remove any air bubbles, screw on the caps, and process them in a boiling-water canner for 10 minutes, or the time recommended for your area by your county extension agent. Cool the jars and press the top of each lid with a finger, ensuring the seal is tight and that the lid does not move up or down at all. (If any jars have not sealed properly, refrigerate them and eat the pickles within 2 weeks.) Store the sealed jars in a cool, dark place for 3–4 weeks before opening. Makes 2 (1-pint) jars.

HOMEMADE TARTAR SAUCE

1 cup	**mayonnaise**
1/4 cup	**finely chopped dill pickle**
2	**green onions,** finely chopped
2 tablespoons	**lemon juice**
1 teaspoon	**chopped fresh dill weed**
	(or 1/2 teaspoon dried dill)
1/4 teaspoon	**salt**
1/4 teaspoon	**pepper**

In a small bowl, whisk together all the ingredients. Serve at room temperature. Store any leftover sauce, tightly covered, in the refrigerator for up to 3 days. Makes about 1 1/2 cups.

THOUSAND ISLAND
SALAD DRESSING

½ cup	**mayonnaise**
½ cup	**ketchup**
1 teaspoon	**Worcestershire sauce**
1 teaspoon	**sugar**
¼ cup	**sweet pickle relish**
1	**hard-boiled egg,** peeled and finely chopped

In a small bowl, whisk together mayonnaise, ketchup, Worcestershire sauce, and sugar. Add relish and chopped egg and stir gently. Store in refrigerator for up to 3 days. Makes about 1 ¼ cups.

PICKLE RANCH
SALAD DRESSING

1 cup	**mayonnaise**
1 cup	**buttermilk**
$1/2$ cup	**finely diced dill pickles**
1 package (1 ounce)	**ranch dressing mix**
$1/4$ cup	**pickle juice**
1 teaspoon	**dried dill**
1 clove	**garlic,** peeled and finely minced

In a food processor or blender, combine the mayonnaise, buttermilk, pickles, ranch dressing mix, pickle juice, dill, and garlic. Process or blend until smooth. Refrigerate for at least 2 hours and stir before serving. Store any leftover dressing, tightly covered, in the refrigerator for up to 3 days. Makes $2^3/4$ cups.

REMOULADE SAUCE

1/3 cup	**finely chopped dill pickles**
1/3 cup	**mayonnaise**
1/4 cup	**sour cream**
2 tablespoons	**finely chopped flat-leaf parsley**
2 tablespoons	**finely chopped shallot**
2 tablespoons	**tomato paste**
1 1/2 teaspoons	**hot pepper sauce**
1 1/2 teaspoons	**fresh lemon juice**

In a small bowl, whisk together all the ingredients. Serve at room temperature with grilled meats, burgers, steamed artichokes, crab cakes, or chilled shrimp, or use as a salad dressing. Store any leftover sauce, tightly covered, in the refrigerator for up to 3 days. Makes about 1 cup.

ZIPPY SWEET PICKLE RELISH

1 teaspoon	**vegetable oil**
1 cup	**finely chopped onion**
3/4 cup	**jalapeno pepper jelly**
1/4 cup	**apple cider vinegar**
2 tablespoons	**sugar**
1/2 teaspoon	**salt**
1 1/2 cups	**finely chopped bread-and-butter pickles**

Heat the oil in a large saucepan over medium heat. Add the onion and cook until translucent, about 10 minutes. Add the jelly, vinegar, sugar, and salt. Increase heat to medium high and bring to a boil. Cook, stirring often, until thickened, about 6 minutes. Remove from heat and cool to room temperature. Stir in pickles and serve. Store any leftover relish, tightly covered, in the refrigerator for up to 1 week. Makes about 2 1/2 cups.

HUNGARIAN PICKLE SAUCE

½ cup	**butter or margarine**
10	**gherkin or mini dill pickles,** finely chopped
1 cup	**chicken, beef, fish, or vegetable stock**
pinch of	**saffron**
2 tablespoons	**sour cream**
2 tablespoons	**flour**
1 teaspoon	**red wine vinegar**
	salt and pepper, to taste

Heat the butter in a medium saucepan, add the pickles, and cook for 5 minutes. Add the stock and bring to a boil. Reduce heat to low, add saffron, and simmer 15 minutes, partially covered.

In a small bowl, combine the sour cream, flour, and vinegar. Add several tablespoons of the hot stock mixture to the sour cream mixture and stir quickly to combine. Add the mixture back to the hot stock, stirring constantly, until the sauce thickens. Season with salt and pepper. Serve with roasted or grilled chicken, beef, or fish, depending on stock used. Makes about 2 cups.

DILL PICKLE GRAVY

2 tablespoons	**butter or margarine**
2 tablespoons	**flour**
1 1/2 cups	**hot beef stock or broth**
3 tablespoons	**sour cream**
2	**dill pickles,** finely grated
	salt and pepper, to taste

In a small saucepan over medium heat, melt the butter and whisk in the flour. Cook, whisking constantly, until mixture begins to brown. Add the stock and continue whisking and cooking until mixture thickens. Stir in the sour cream and pickles until smooth. Remove from heat and season with salt and pepper. Serve as an accompaniment to beef and potato dishes. Makes about 2 cups.

PICKLE DIPPING SAUCE

¹/₂ cup	**mayonnaise**
¹/₂ cup	**sour cream**
¹/₂ cup	**minced dill pickles**
1 ¹/₂ teaspoons	**dried dill**
¹/₄ teaspoon	**garlic powder**
¹/₄ teaspoon	**salt**
¹/₄ teaspoon	**pepper**

Combine all ingredients in a small bowl. Cover tightly and refrigerate for at least 2 hours to allow flavors to meld; stir before serving. Serve as a dipping sauce with French fries, chicken tenders, fish sticks, raw vegetables, and chips. Store any leftover sauce, tightly covered, in the refrigerator for up to 3 days. Makes 1 ¹/₂ cups.

CORNICHON-MUSTARD SAUCE

1/3 cup	**mayonnaise**
1/3 cup	**sour cream**
1/4 cup	**finely chopped cornichons or baby dill pickles**
2 tablespoons	**whole-grain mustard**
1/4 teaspoon	**dried dill**
	salt and pepper, to taste

In a small bowl, whisk together the mayonnaise, sour cream, cornichons, mustard, and dill. Season with salt and pepper. Use as a sandwich condiment or a sauce for grilled meats. Store any leftover sauce, tightly covered, in the refrigerator for up to 3 days. Makes about 1 cup.

PICKLE COMPOUND BUTTER

4 tablespoons	**butter or margarine,** softened
¹/₄ cup	**finely diced dill pickles**
1 teaspoon	**minced fresh tarragon**
¹/₂ teaspoon	**Dijon mustard**
	salt and pepper, to taste

In a small bowl, blend the butter with the pickles, tarragon, and mustard. Season with salt and pepper. Using a spatula, scoop the mixture onto a large piece of plastic wrap and shape into a log. Wrap tightly and twist the ends to seal. Refrigerate until firm, about 3 hours.

To serve, cut into 8 equal slices. Place 1 slice per serving on hot grilled fish, poultry, or meats. Makes 8 servings.

APPETIZERS & SNACKS

DILL PICKLE DIP

8 ounces	**cream cheese,** softened
2 tablespoons	**dill pickle juice**
2	**medium dill pickles,** finely chopped
2 tablespoons	**finely chopped onion**
I teaspoon	**dried dill**
1/4 teaspoon	**salt**
	potato chips

In a small bowl, combine the cream cheese and pickle juice and stir until blended. Add the pickles, onion, dill, and salt and stir well. Cover and chill for I hour. Serve with chips. Store any leftover dip, tightly covered, in the refrigerator for up to 3 days. Makes 1 1/3 cups.

BACON-WRAPPED PICKLE POPPERS

I jar (16 ounces)	**baby dill pickles**
4 ounces	**cream cheese,** softened
I cup	**grated cheddar cheese**
I pound	**sliced bacon**

Preheat oven broiler and arrange the broiler rack about 4 inches from heat. Line a baking sheet with aluminum foil; prepare with nonstick cooking spray and reserve.

Drain pickles and blot with paper towels to absorb moisture. In a small bowl, combine the cream cheese and cheddar cheese and stir until combined. Cut the bacon strips in half widthwise.

Using a sharp knife, cut a pickle in half lengthwise and cut a small wedge from the center. Spread both halves with some of the cream cheese mixture and press together. Wrap with a strip of bacon and secure with a toothpick. Repeat with remaining pickles, cheese mixture, and bacon. Arrange the bacon-wrapped pickles on the prepared baking sheet. Broil the pickles, turning once during cooking, until the bacon is crispy and browned, about 8–10 minutes. Makes 24–30 appetizers.

SOUTHERN-FRIED PICKLES

I cup	**flour**
¼ cup	**cornstarch**
I teaspoon	**baking powder**
¼ teaspoon	**salt**
I cup	**ice water**
I	**egg yolk**
2 tablespoons	**dill pickle juice**
4 cups	**drained round dill pickle slices**
	vegetable oil
	ranch dressing

Stir flour, cornstarch, baking powder, and salt into a large bowl. Make a well in center and add the water, egg yolk, and pickle juice all at once. Whisk to make a smooth batter. Cover bowl and refrigerate for 30 minutes.

In a deep fryer or large saucepan, heat 2 inches of oil to 365 degrees. In batches, dip pickle slices into the batter, coating lightly and evenly. Fry, without crowding in hot oil, until golden and crisp, 1½–2 minutes. Drain on paper towels and serve with ranch dressing. Makes 8 servings.

BATTER-FRIED PICKLE SPEARS WITH SPICY RANCH

⅓ cup	**ranch dressing**
1–2 teaspoons	**hot pepper sauce**
1 jar (24 ounces)	**dill pickle spears**
1½ cups	**flour**
1 teaspoon	**garlic powder**
½ teaspoon	**salt**
¼ teaspoon	**paprika**
¼ teaspoon	**pepper**
2	**eggs**
¾ cup	**club soda**
1 tablespoon	**melted butter or margarine**
	vegetable oil

In a small bowl, combine the ranch dressing and hot pepper sauce to taste; cover and refrigerate. Drain pickles, reserving 2 tablespoons pickle juice. Cut each pickle spear in half lengthwise and arrange on a paper towel-lined baking sheet; cover and refrigerate.

Whisk together the flour, garlic powder, salt, paprika, and pepper in a medium bowl. Separate the eggs and beat the egg yolks. (Reserve and refrigerate the egg whites.) Add the egg yolks, club soda, butter, and reserved pickle juice to flour mixture and stir just until combined; a few lumps are okay. Refrigerate batter, covered, for 1 hour. In a medium bowl, beat the egg whites until stiff; fold the whites into the batter mixture.

Pour oil to a depth of 3 inches in a large heavy saucepan or Dutch oven and heat to 365 degrees. Dip pickles into batter, letting excess drip off, and fry in batches for 2–3 minutes, turning once, until golden brown. Drain on paper towels and serve with spicy ranch sauce. Makes 6 servings.

OVEN-FRIED PICKLES

6 (4-inch)	**dill pickles,** cut into 1/2-inch slices
2	**eggs**
1/3 cup	**flour**
1 tablespoon	**Worcestershire sauce**
1 teaspoon	**hot sauce**
1 teaspoon	**garlic powder**
1 teaspoon	**Cajun seasoning**
1 teaspoon	**pepper**
1 1/2 cups	**panko breadcrumbs**
2 tablespoons	**olive oil**
	ranch dressing

Preheat oven to 400 degrees and line a baking sheet with aluminum foil; prepare with nonstick cooking spray and reserve. Drain the pickle slices and blot with paper towels to dry.

In a medium bowl, whisk together the eggs and flour. Add the Worcestershire sauce, hot sauce, garlic powder, Cajun seasoning, and pepper and mix well. Pour the breadcrumbs into a shallow dish. Dunk each pickle slice into the egg mixture, and then into the breadcrumbs. Arrange on the prepared baking sheet, leaving at least 1/2 inch between slices.

Drizzle the pickles lightly with 1 tablespoon olive oil. Bake for 8 minutes, then flip each pickle, drizzle with remaining oil, and bake for another 8 minutes or until golden brown. Serve with ranch dressing. Makes 48 appetizers.

PICKLE PIMIENTO CHEESE TOASTS

2 cups	**grated sharp cheddar cheese**
4 ounces	**cream cheese,** softened
$^1/_2$ cup	**mayonnaise**
1 jar (4 ounces)	**diced pimientos,** drained
3 tablespoons	**minced dill pickle**
$^1/_2$ teaspoon	**pepper**
$^1/_4$ teaspoon	**salt**
$^1/_4$ teaspoon	**garlic powder**
$^1/_4$ teaspoon	**paprika**
9 slices	**bread**
6	**baby dill pickles,** each cut into 6 slices

Combine the cheese, cream cheese, mayonnaise, pimientos, minced pickle, pepper, salt, garlic powder, and paprika in a food processor or mixing bowl. Process or mix just until well blended. Cover and refrigerate for at least 1 hour.

Toast the bread and cut each slice into 4 squares. Spread with the pimiento cheese and top with a pickle slice. Makes 36 appetizers.

PICKLE PARTY BREAD

8 ounces	**cream cheese,** softened
I can (6 ounces)	**chopped black olives**
I ½ teaspoons	**garlic powder**
I tablespoon	**dill pickle juice**
I (18-inch) loaf	**baguette bread**
6 (3-inch)	**dill pickles**

In a medium bowl, combine the cream cheese, olives, garlic powder, and pickle juice until well blended.

Slice off both ends of the baguette. Lay a pickle next to the loaf and slice the bread the same length as the pickle. Remove the bread from the center of each length of bread, leaving ½ inch around the edges. Spread the inside of the hollow bread pieces with the cream cheese mixture and stuff a pickle in the center, using a knife to add more of the cream cheese mixture if necessary. Wrap tightly in plastic wrap and repeat with remaining pickles, bread, and cream cheese mixture.

Refrigerate the wrapped bread sections for at least 2 hours. Remove from refrigerator, unwrap, and cut each section into ½-inch slices. Makes 36 appetizers.

CRISPY PICKLE EGG ROLLS

12 (3-inch)	**pickle spears**
12	**eggroll wrappers**
12 slices	**dill Havarti cheese**
1/4 cup	**olive oil,** divided

Preheat oven to 400 degrees and line a baking sheet with aluminum foil; prepare with nonstick cooking spray and reserve. Drain the pickle spears and blot with paper towels to dry.

Keep the egg roll wrappers covered with plastic wrap. Lay 1 wrapper on a work surface and lightly wet edges with water. Place a slice of cheese in the center of the wrapper and top diagonally with a pickle spear. Fold in the two corners over the spear ends, fold up the bottom corner over the spear, and roll up tightly like an envelope, placing seam side down on the prepared baking sheet. Repeat with remaining wrappers, cheese, and pickles. Brush the rolls with half the olive oil and bake for 10 minutes. Turn over, brush with remaining oil, and continue baking another 8–10 minutes, or until golden and crispy. Makes 12 appetizers.

DILLY HUMMUS

1 can (15 ounces)	**garbanzo beans,** drained
1 clove	**garlic,** peeled and minced
2	**whole dill pickles,** chopped
3 tablespoons	**dill pickle juice**
2 tablespoons	**olive oil**
2 teaspoons	**chopped fresh dill weed** (or $1/2$ teaspoon dried dill)
	crackers or raw sliced vegetables

In a food processor, combine the garbanzo beans, garlic, pickles, pickle juice, olive oil, and dill and process until smooth. Serve with crackers or vegetables. Makes 6 servings.

PICKLE PASTRAMI ROLL-UPS

8 slices	**deli pastrami**
	(or sliced ham)
8 (4-inch)	**whole dill pickles**
8 ounces	**cream cheese,** softened
	assorted crackers

Pat the pastrami and pickles dry with paper towels. Spread a thin layer of cream cheese on each pastrami slice. Place a pickle at one end and roll tightly like a jelly roll. Secure with toothpicks and refrigerate for 2 hours. Slice the rolls into 1-inch pieces and serve with crackers. Makes 32 appetizers.

CRISPY CRAB CAKES

¹/₂ cup	**mayonnaise**
1	**egg,** beaten
1 tablespoon	**Worcestershire sauce**
1 tablespoon	**Dijon mustard**
1 teaspoon	**seafood seasoning** (Old Bay)
¹/₂ teaspoon	**hot pepper sauce**
1 pound	**jumbo lump crabmeat,** picked through for shells
20	**saltine crackers,** finely crushed
6	**baby dill pickles,** finely chopped
¹/₄ cup	**vegetable oil**
1	**lemon,** cut in 8 wedges

In a small bowl, whisk together the mayonnaise, egg, Worcestershire sauce, mustard, seafood seasoning, and hot sauce until smooth.

In a medium bowl, lightly toss the crabmeat with the cracker crumbs and chopped pickles. Add the mayonnaise mixture and stir gently. Cover and refrigerate for 1 hour.

Scoop the crab mixture into 8 (¹/₃-cup) mounds and lightly pack into 8 patties, about 1 ¹/₂ inches thick. In a large frying pan, heat the oil over medium-high heat until shimmering. Add the crab cakes and cook until golden brown and cooked through, about 3 minutes per side. Serve with lemon wedges. Makes 8 crab cakes.

NEON STATE-FAIR PICKLES

1 gallon jar	**whole dill pickles**
2 cups	**sugar**
2 packages	**unsweetened powdered drink mix,** such as Kool-Aid, cherry flavor or flavor of your choice

Pour the brine from the pickles into a large bowl. Add the sugar and powdered drink mix to the brine and stir until dissolved.

Cut the pickles in half lengthwise and replace in the jar. Pour the brine mixture over the pickles to the top of the jar (you may have extra). Refrigerate for 1 week. Makes 1 gallon.

JO ANNE'S HOT SWEET PICKLES

1 gallon jar	**whole dill pickles**
$3/4$ pound	**jalapeno peppers** (or $1/2$ pound Anaheim chiles for milder pickles)
5 cups	**sugar**

Drain the brine from the pickles and reserve. Cut the peppers in half lengthwise, remove seeds and stems, and cut in $1/4$-inch slices. Add the sugar and peppers to the pickle jar and enough brine to fill to within 2 inches of the top. Replace the lid and shake until the sugar is dissolved. Each day for the following 6 days, shake the jar well. The pickles are ready to eat on the seventh day. Store in the refrigerator and eat within 2 months. Makes 1 gallon.

BEEF AND PICKLE CHEESE SPREAD

3 cups	**grated Monterey Jack cheese**
3/4 cup	**chopped thinly sliced dried beef or deli corned beef**
2/3 cup	**mayonnaise**
1 cup	**finely chopped dill pickles,** divided
8 ounces	**cream cheese,** softened
1/4 teaspoon	**pepper**
1/4 teaspoon	**garlic powder**
	assorted crackers

In a large bowl, combine the cheese, chopped beef, mayonnaise, 3/4 cup chopped pickles, cream cheese, pepper, and garlic powder. Cover and chill for at least 2 hours or overnight. Before serving, garnish with remaining 1/4 cup chopped pickles. Serve with crackers. Makes 8–10 servings.

FRESH TOMATO AND PICKLE SALSA

2	**large tomatoes,** chopped
1/2 cup	**chopped dill pickles**
1	**Anaheim pepper,** seeded and finely chopped
1	**jalapeno pepper,** seeded and finely chopped
1/4 cup	**finely chopped red onion**
2 tablespoons	**olive oil**
1 tablespoon	**red wine vinegar**
1 tablespoon	**minced fresh cilantro**
2 teaspoons	**dill pickle juice**
1/4 teaspoon	**salt**
1/4 teaspoon	**pepper**
	tortilla or corn chips

In a small bowl, combine the tomatoes, pickles, peppers, onion, olive oil, vinegar, cilantro, pickle juice, salt, and pepper. Cover and refrigerate for at least 2 hours. Serve with tortilla or corn chips. Makes 6 servings.

DILL PICKLE CHEESE BALL

8 ounces	**cream cheese,** softened
1 cup	**grated cheddar cheese**
1/2 cup	**chopped dill pickles**
1/2 cup	**chopped deli salami**
2 tablespoons	**mayonnaise**
1 teaspoon	**Worcestershire sauce**
1/4 teaspoon	**pepper**
1/3 cup	**cracker crumbs**
1 tablespoon	**finely chopped fresh parsley**
1/2 teaspoon	**dried dill**
	assorted crackers

In a large bowl, mix the cream cheese, cheddar cheese, pickles, salami, mayonnaise, Worcestershire sauce, and pepper until smooth. Cover and refrigerate for 2 hours, or until firm. Uncover and shape mixture into a ball. Combine cracker crumbs, parsley, and dill in a shallow dish. Roll the cheese ball in the mixture to cover completely. Serve on a platter accompanied by crackers. Makes 8 servings.

MINI GRILLED CORNED BEEF, PICKLE, AND CHEESE SANDWICHES

24 slices	**cocktail-size pumpernickel bread**
24 slices	**Swiss cheese,** cut to fit bread
I cup	**dill pickle slices,** blotted dry with paper towels
$1/8$ pound	**thin-sliced corned beef,** cut to fit bread
2 tablespoons	**butter or margarine,** divided
I tablespoon	**vegetable oil,** divided

On each of 12 slices of bread, divide half of the cheese slices and arrange on the bread. Cover with a layer of pickle slices. Divide the corned beef slices and arrange on top, followed by the remaining cheese slices. Top with the remaining 12 bread slices.

Heat I tablespoon butter and I $1/2$ teaspoons vegetable oil in a large frying pan over medium heat. Add half of the sandwiches and cook until crispy, 2–3 minutes. Flip over and cook the other sides until crispy. Wipe out the pan, heat the remaining butter and vegetable oil, and cook the remaining sandwiches. Cut each sandwich in half diagonally. Makes 24 appetizers.

CUBANITOS

2 tablespoons	**butter or margarine,** melted
I clove	**garlic,** peeled and minced
4	**ciabatta rolls,** split
2 tablespoons	**prepared mustard**
8 slices	**Swiss cheese**
8	**dill pickle sandwich slices**
8 ounces	**thinly sliced deli roast pork**
8 slices	**crispy cooked bacon**

In a small bowl, combine the butter and garlic. Brush the outsides of the rolls with the mixture. Spread the insides of the rolls with mustard and reserve the top halves. Put the bottom halves of the rolls on a work surface, butter side down, and top each with I cheese slice and 2 pickles. Divide pork evenly among the rolls and top each with 2 pieces crumbled bacon and another slice of cheese. Replace roll tops butter side up, and press gently together.

Heat a large frying pan over medium heat. Add the sandwiches and weigh down with another heavy frying pan. Cook 2–3 minutes or until bread is golden brown; flip over and cook the other sides until golden brown. Remove to a cutting board and use a sharp knife to cut each sandwich into 4 squares. Makes 16 appetizers.

SOUPS &
SALADS

DILL PICKLE SOUP

1/2 cup	**butter or margarine**
1/4 cup	**finely chopped onion**
1/4 cup	**flour**
3 1/2 cups	**chicken broth**
3/4 cup	**finely chopped dill pickles**
1 clove	**garlic,** minced
1 teaspoon	**dried dill**
3/4 teaspoon	**salt**
1/4 teaspoon	**white pepper**
1 cup	**half-and-half**

In a large, heavy saucepan, melt the butter over medium heat. Add the onion and cook for 2–3 minutes, just until translucent. Whisk in the flour until smooth. Gradually add the broth, stirring constantly, until thickened and smooth.

Add the pickles, garlic, dill, salt, and pepper, and cook until soup just starts to bubble. Add the half-and-half and cook, stirring constantly, until mixture just starts to bubble. Adjust seasonings, if necessary, and serve. Makes 4–6 servings.

SUMMER GAZPACHO

I clove	**garlic,** peeled
¹/₂ cup	**chopped dill pickles**
¹/₂ cup	**peeled, seeded, and cubed cucumber**
¹/₂ cup	**chopped yellow bell pepper**
¹/₂ cup	**chopped tomato**
¹/₄ cup	**chopped peeled carrot**
I can (4.25 ounces)	**sliced black olives,** drained
2	**green onions,** sliced
¹/₄ cup	**chopped fresh parsley**
6 teaspoons	**olive oil**
2 teaspoons	**lemon juice**
I teaspoon	**sugar**
¹/₂ teaspoon	**salt**
¹/₄ teaspoon	**pepper**
4 cups	**beef broth**

Cut the garlic in half and rub the inside of a glass salad bowl with it. Add the pickles, cucumber, bell pepper, tomato, carrot, olives, green onions, and parsley to the bowl, and drizzle with the olive oil and lemon juice. Sprinkle with sugar, salt, and pepper. Add the broth, stir, cover, and chill in refrigerator for several hours. Makes 6 servings.

SAVORY SEAFOOD SOUP

I tablespoon	**olive oil**
$^1/_2$ cup	**chopped onion**
$^1/_2$ cup	**chopped green bell pepper**
$^1/_2$ teaspoon	**minced garlic**
I can (14 ounces)	**diced tomatoes with liquid**
I jar (14 ounces)	**spaghetti sauce**
I cup	**salsa**
I cup	**chicken broth**
$^1/_2$ cup	**chopped dill pickles**
$^1/_4$ cup	**dill pickle juice**
$^1/_4$ teaspoon	**dried oregano**
$^1/_4$ teaspoon	**dried basil**
$^1/_4$ teaspoon	**pepper**
$^3/_4$ pound	**shrimp,** peeled and deveined
$^3/_4$ pound	**lump crabmeat or 2 cans (6 ounces each) crabmeat,** drained and picked through for any bits of shell
I can (6.5 ounces)	**minced clams with liquid**
2 tablespoons	**chopped flat-leaf parsley**

Heat the olive oil in a Dutch oven over medium heat, and cook the onion and bell pepper until onion is tender, about 5 minutes. Add garlic and cook I minute longer. Stir in the tomatoes, spaghetti sauce, salsa, broth, pickles, pickle juice, oregano, basil, and pepper. Increase heat to medium-high and bring to a boil. Reduce heat; cover and simmer for 20 minutes.

Add the shrimp, crab, and clams. Cover and simmer for 5–6 minutes, or until shrimp turn pink and are cooked through. Ladle into heated bowls and garnish with chopped parsley. Makes 8 servings.

HOT AND SOUR SOUP

3 tablespoons	**cornstarch**
3 tablespoons	**rice vinegar**
3 $^1/_2$ cups	**chicken broth**
1 cup	**sliced fresh mushrooms**
$^3/_4$ cup	**chopped dill pickles**
$^1/_2$ cup	**sliced canned bamboo shoots**
$^1/_4$ cup	**chopped onion**
2 cloves	**garlic,** peeled and crushed
2 teaspoons	**soy sauce**
$^1/_4$ teaspoon	**red pepper flakes**
1 pound	**boneless, skinless chicken breasts,** cut into $^1/_2$-inch strips
1	**egg,** beaten
2	**green onions,** chopped

In a small bowl, stir together the cornstarch and vinegar; set aside. In a large saucepan, combine the broth, mushrooms, pickles, bamboo shoots, onion, garlic, soy sauce and pepper flakes. Bring to a boil, reduce heat to low, cover, and simmer for 10 minutes.

Remove the cover, increase the heat to medium-high, and bring to a rolling boil. Add the chicken and return to a boil. Drizzle in the egg while stirring slowly to create long strands. Stir in the vinegar and cornstarch mixture. Simmer over medium heat, stirring occasionally, until chicken is cooked through and the broth has thickened slightly, about 3 minutes. Serve garnished with green onions. Makes 6 servings.

DILLICIOUS BEAN CHOWDER

1 1/4 cups	**dried navy beans,** rinsed
6 cups	**water**
1 1/2 cups	**sliced dill pickles**
1 can (28 ounces)	**diced tomatoes with juice**
2 cups	**beef broth**
1/4 cup	**dill pickle juice**
1 cup	**sliced celery**
1 cup	**thinly sliced cabbage**
2	**carrots,** peeled and thinly sliced
1	**small onion,** chopped
1 clove	**garlic,** minced
1 teaspoon	**salt**
1/2 teaspoon	**dried dill**
1/8 teaspoon	**pepper**

Put the beans in a large heavy saucepan and add enough water to cover. Bring to a boil over medium-high heat and cook for 2 minutes. Remove from heat, cover, and let beans soak for 1 hour.

Drain the beans, reserving the cooking liquid. Pour the beans and 2 cups of the liquid back into the pot and add the remaining ingredients. Cook over medium heat until mixture boils. Reduce heat to low, cover, and simmer 1 1/2–2 hours, adding reserved bean liquid, as needed. Stir occasionally until beans are tender. Makes 8 servings.

SWEET PICKLE DEVILED EGG SALAD

$3/4$ cup	**mayonnaise**
$1/3$ cup	**finely chopped sweet pickles or sweet pickle relish**
$1/4$ cup	**finely diced celery**
1 teaspoon	**prepared mustard**
$1/4$ teaspoon	**salt**
$1/4$ teaspoon	**pepper**
12	**hard-boiled eggs,** peeled and chopped
6	**butter lettuce leaves**

In a medium bowl, combine the mayonnaise, sweet pickles or relish, celery, mustard, salt, and pepper. Add the chopped eggs and stir gently to combine. Cover and refrigerate for 2 hours. Arrange a lettuce leaf on each of 6 chilled salad plates and divide the salad evenly among the plates. Makes 6 servings.

MARINATED BEEF, PICKLE, AND AVOCADO SALAD

1/2 cup	**peanut oil**
1/4 cup	**olive oil**
1/2 cup	**red wine vinegar**
2 teaspoons	**Dijon mustard**
1 teaspoon	**salt**
1/2 teaspoon	**pepper**
2 pounds	**cooked, sliced roast beef**
1	**small head butter lettuce,** washed, dried, and leaves separated
18	**dill pickle sandwich slices**
2	**ripe avocados,** peeled and sliced
1	**small red onion,** sliced into thin rings
1/4 cup	**chopped flat-leaf parsley**

In a small bowl, make a dressing by combining the peanut oil, olive oil, vinegar, mustard, salt, and pepper; whisk to blend. Cut the beef into 1-inch slices and transfer to a container. Drizzle all but 1/4 cup of the dressing over the beef and toss to coat. Cover and refrigerate the beef mixture and reserved dressing for 2 hours.

Arrange the lettuce leaves around the outer edge of a serving platter, tearing, if necessary, to fit. Transfer the marinated beef to the center of the platter. Cut each dill pickle slice in vertical strips. Arrange the pickle slices, avocado slices, and onion slices around the meat. Drizzle with the remaining dressing and sprinkle with chopped parsley. Makes 6 servings.

CHICKLE PICKEN SALAD

3 cups	**chopped cooked chicken**
1/2 cup	**diced, drained bread-and-butter pickles**
1/2 cup	**finely chopped celery**
3/4 cup	**mayonnaise**
1/2 package (1 ounce)	**ranch dip mix**
1 tablespoon	**minced fresh dill weed** (or 1 teaspoon dried dill)
1 teaspoon	**lemon juice**
	salt and pepper, to taste
6	**red lettuce leaves**
6	**bread-and-butter pickle slices,** drained and cut into thin strips

In a large bowl, mix together the chicken, pickles, and celery. In a small bowl, whisk together the mayonnaise, ranch dip mix, dill, and lemon juice. Add salt and pepper, and whisk to combine.

Arrange a lettuce leaf on each of 6 chilled salad plates and divide the salad evenly among the plates; garnish with pickle strips. Makes 6 servings.

ZIPPY COLESLAW

$^2/_3$ cup	**mayonnaise**
I tablespoon	**balsamic vinegar**
2 teaspoons	**sugar**
$^1/_4$ cup	**dill pickle juice**
$^1/_2$ teaspoon	**dry mustard**
$^1/_2$ teaspoon	**pepper**
$^1/_4$ teaspoon	**salt**
3 cups	**shredded green cabbage**
I cup	**shredded red cabbage**
3	**medium carrots,** peeled and grated
3	**medium dill pickles,** diced

In a large bowl, whisk together the mayonnaise, vinegar, sugar, pickle juice, mustard, pepper, and salt. Add the cabbage, carrots, and pickles and toss gently. Serve at once or cover and refrigerate. Makes 8 servings.

OLD-FASHIONED POTATO SALAD

3 pounds	**potatoes,** peeled and diced
1 1/2 cups	**mayonnaise**
1/4 cup	**dill pickle juice**
1 tablespoon	**prepared mustard**
1 teaspoon	**celery seeds**
3	**medium dill pickles,** finely chopped
3	**hard-boiled eggs,** peeled and chopped
3	**celery stalks,** chopped
3	**green onions,** chopped
	salt and pepper, to taste

Place potatoes in a large pot and fill with enough water to cover. Bring to a boil and cook for 10–15 minutes, or until easily pierced with a fork; drain and set aside to cool.

In a large bowl, whisk together the mayonnaise, pickle juice, mustard, and celery seeds. Add the potatoes, pickles, eggs, celery, and green onions. Stir gently to combine, and season with salt and pepper. Cover and refrigerate for at least 4 hours. Makes 8–10 servings.

GERMAN POTATO PICKLE SALAD

1/4 cup	**white wine vinegar**
1 tablespoon	**whole-grain mustard**
3 teaspoons	**salt,** divided
1/2 teaspoon	**pepper**
1/4 cup	**olive oil**
1/4 cup	**rice vinegar**
3 1/2 pounds	**medium red or Yukon Gold potatoes,** peeled and cut into 3/4-inch cubes
3/4 pound	**bacon**
1	**large onion,** diced
3/4 cup	**diced dill pickles**
1/2 cup	**finely chopped flat-leaf parsley**

Combine the white wine vinegar, mustard, 1 teaspoon salt, and pepper in a small bowl. Slowly whisk in the oil until combined.

Combine the rice vinegar and remaining 2 teaspoons salt in a large bowl and set aside. Place the potatoes in a pot and fill with enough water to cover. Bring to a boil and cook for about 10 minutes, or until easily pierced with a fork. Drain and add the warm potatoes to the rice vinegar mixture. Stir gently.

Fry the bacon in a large frying pan over medium-high heat until browned and crisp. Remove the bacon, drain, and crumble. Add the onion to the bacon drippings and cook over medium heat until browned. Add the onions, bacon, pickles, and parsley to the potatoes and stir gently. Whisk the dressing, drizzle it over the salad (you may not need all of it), and stir to combine. Adjust seasonings, if needed; serve warm. Makes 6 servings.

PICKLE CUCUMBER MINT SALAD

2 tablespoons	**olive oil**
2 tablespoons	**lemon juice**
$1/2$ teaspoon	**salt**
$1/4$ teaspoon	**pepper**
2	**large English cucumbers,** peeled and diced
2 pounds	**ripe tomatoes,** seeded and diced
6	**large dill pickles,** diced
$1/4$ cup	**chopped fresh mint**
2 cups	**mixed greens**

In a large bowl, whisk together the olive oil, lemon juice, salt, and pepper. Add the cucumbers, tomatoes, pickles, and mint. Stir gently and adjust seasonings, if needed.

Divide the mixed greens among 6 chilled salad plates and mound the salad on top of each plate. Makes 6 servings.

PICKLE KIDNEY BEAN SALAD

2 cans (15 ounces)	**kidney beans,** drained
$1/2$ cup	**chopped, drained bread-and-butter pickles**
$1/2$ cup	**mayonnaise**
$1/2$	**small red onion,** diced
2	**celery stalks,** diced
2	**hard-boiled eggs,** peeled and chopped
	salt and pepper, to taste

In a large bowl, combine the beans, pickles, mayonnaise, onion, celery, and eggs and stir gently. Season with salt and pepper. Chill at least 1 hour in the refrigerator before serving. Makes 6 servings.

PICKLE PASTA SALAD

12 ounces	**uncooked spiral pasta**
1/2 cup	**Italian salad dressing**
6	**baby dill pickles,** cut into 1/4-inch slices
1	**large tomato,** chopped
1	**medium red bell pepper,** chopped
1/3 cup	**chopped celery**
1 can (2.25 ounces)	**sliced black olives,** drained
1/4 cup	**finely chopped flat-leaf parsley**
1/4 cup	**shredded Parmesan cheese**
	salt and pepper, to taste

Bring a large pot of lightly salted water to a boil and add the pasta. Cook according to package directions, drain, cool briefly, and then add to a large salad bowl. Add the dressing and mix gently. Add the pickles, tomato, bell pepper, celery, and black olives. Cover and chill for at least 1 hour in the refrigerator. Add the chopped parsley and Parmesan and stir gently to combine. Season with salt and pepper. Makes 6 servings.

CUBAN CHICKEN SALAD

3 cups	**chopped romaine lettuce**
2 cups	**chopped cooked chicken**
³/₄ cup	**diced dill pickles**
³/₄ cup	**canned black beans,** drained
I	**small red onion,** diced
I	**avocado,** peeled and diced
¹/₂ cup	**chopped, drained roasted red bell pepper**
2 tablespoons	**olive oil**
I clove	**garlic,** peeled and minced
I tablespoon	**lime juice**
	salt and pepper, to taste

Toss the lettuce with the chicken, pickles, beans, onion, avocado, and bell pepper in a large bowl. In a small bowl, whisk together the olive oil, garlic, and lime juice. Drizzle the dressing over the salad and toss gently. Season with salt and pepper. Makes 6 servings.

SHRIMPICKLE SALAD

1 pound	**cooked, peeled extra-small shrimp**
½ cup	**finely chopped dill pickles,** well drained
½ cup	**finely chopped celery**
2 tablespoons	**finely chopped sweet onion**
¼ teaspoon	**pepper**
½ cup	**mayonnaise**
1½ teaspoons	**fresh lemon juice**
2	**hard-boiled eggs,** peeled and chopped
4	**butter lettuce leaves**

Mix together the shrimp, pickles, celery, onion, and pepper. Add the mayonnaise and lemon juice; stir to combine. Gently fold in the eggs. Arrange a lettuce leaf on each of 4 chilled salad plates and divide the salad evenly among the plates. Makes 4 servings.

CHILLED PICKLES AND TOMATOES WITH WARM BEARNAISE SAUCE

2 pounds	**ripe garden tomatoes**
8	**medium dill pickles**
2 tablespoons	**white wine vinegar**
2 tablespoons	**white wine**
1	**small shallot,** minced
2 teaspoons	**minced tarragon leaves,** divided
1 teaspoon	**lemon juice**
1/2 teaspoon	**salt,** divided
1/4 teaspoon	**pepper**
3	**egg yolks**
1/2 cup	**butter or margarine**

Slice the tomatoes and pickles into 1/4-inch-thick rounds and drain them on paper towels. Arrange the slices overlapping slightly on a serving platter; cover and refrigerate for 2 hours.

In a small saucepan, combine the vinegar, wine, shallot, 1 teaspoon tarragon, lemon juice, 1/4 teaspoon salt, and pepper. Bring to a boil over medium-high heat; reduce heat to medium and simmer for 5 minutes. Remove from heat and cool for several minutes.

In a blender, combine the egg yolks, the remaining salt, and the shallot-wine mixture; blend for 30 seconds. In a small saucepan, melt the butter over medium heat. Turn the blender on and drizzle the hot, melted butter into the shallot mixture in a slow stream. Add the remaining tarragon leaves and pulse briefly to blend.

Drizzle the warm sauce over the sliced tomatoes and pickles and serve at once. Makes 4 servings.

MACARONI, PICKLE, AND HAM SALAD

4 cups	**uncooked elbow macaroni**
I cup	**chopped dill pickles**
I cup	**diced cooked ham**
I block (7 ounces)	**Colby cheese,** diced
3	**hard-boiled eggs,** peeled and chopped
2	**green onions,** finely chopped
³/₄ cup	**mayonnaise**
I tablespoon	**Dijon mustard**

Bring a large pot of lightly salted water to a boil and add the pasta. Cook according to package directions, drain, and briefly cool. Transfer to a large salad bowl. Add the pickles, ham, cheese, eggs, and green onions; gently stir.

In a small bowl, whisk together the mayonnaise and mustard until combined. Add to the macaroni mixture and gently fold to coat with dressing. Cover and chill for at least I hour before serving. Makes 6 servings.

DANISH COBB SALAD

2	**medium potatoes,** peeled and cut into $1/2$-inch cubes
I head	**romaine lettuce,** torn into bite-size pieces
I head	**butter lettuce,** torn into bite-size pieces
8	**medium (3-inch) dill pickles,** cut into $1/4$-inch slices
I pound	**large cooked shrimp,** peeled, deveined, and cut into $1/2$-inch pieces
2	**ripe avocados,** peeled and diced
4	**hard-boiled eggs,** peeled and chopped
24	**cherry tomatoes,** halved
$1/2$ teaspoon	**salt**
$1/4$ teaspoon	**pepper**
$1/2$ cup	**blue cheese dressing**

Bring a large pot of lightly salted water to a boil and add the potatoes. Cook until just tender, drain, and cool.

Combine the romaine and butter lettuces in a large salad bowl and toss gently. Add the cooled potatoes, pickles, shrimp, avocados, eggs, and cherry tomatoes. Sprinkle with salt and pepper and toss gently to combine. Drizzle with $1/4$ cup dressing and toss gently. Add additional dressing, to taste, and serve. Makes 6 servings.

DELUXE CHEESEBURGER SALAD

2 teaspoons	**vegetable oil**
I	**small onion,** diced
2 cloves	**garlic,** peeled and minced
¹/₂ pound	**lean ground beef**
2 tablespoons	**ketchup**
2 teaspoons	**prepared mustard**
I teaspoon	**Worcestershire sauce**
¹/₄ teaspoon	**salt**
¹/₄ teaspoon	**pepper**
2 tablespoons	**butter or margarine**
2	**hamburger buns,** toasted and cut into I-inch cubes
I head	**romaine lettuce,** torn into bite-size pieces
2	**large tomatoes,** diced
I cup	**diced dill pickles**
I cup	**grated mild cheddar cheese**
¹/₄ pound	**bacon,** cooked and crumbled
	Thousand Island Salad Dressing (see recipe on page 22)

Heat oil in a medium frying pan over medium heat and cook onion until tender, about 5 minutes. Add garlic and cook, about I minute. Add ground beef and cook until no longer pink. Drain grease from the pan and add the ketchup, mustard, Worcestershire sauce, salt, and pepper. Heat to simmering and cook for 5 minutes to thicken. Remove from heat and adjust seasonings; set aside.

Melt butter in a large frying pan over medium-high heat and add the cubed buns. Cook, stirring frequently, until lightly browned and crispy. Transfer croutons to paper towels and cool. In a large bowl, toss the lettuce, tomatoes, beef mixture, croutons, pickles, cheese, and bacon. Drizzle with dressing, to taste. Makes 4–6 servings.

TRIPLE GREEN SALAD

2 teaspoons	**olive oil**
2 teaspoons	**balsamic vinegar**
$1/2$ pound	**cooked green beans,** cut into 1-inch pieces
$3/4$ cup	**diced dill pickles**
$1/4$ cup	**diced red onion**
12	**pimiento-stuffed green olives,** sliced
	salt and pepper, to taste

Whisk together olive oil and vinegar in a medium bowl. Add green beans, pickles, onion, and olives and stir gently. Season with salt and pepper. Cover and refrigerate for 30 minutes, stirring occasionally to blend flavors. Makes 6 servings.

SANDWICHES

CHEESY PICKLE PANINI WITH ROAST BEEF

8 slices	**sourdough bread**
3 tablespoons	**butter or margarine,** melted
4 tablespoons	**mayonnaise**
1 pound	**thinly sliced roast beef**
8 slices	**Monterey Jack cheese**
12	**dill pickle sandwich slices**
	salt and pepper, to taste

Brush one side of bread slices generously with melted butter. Flip bread slices over and spread with mayonnaise. Divide the roast beef among 4 bread slices and top each with 2 slices cheese and 3 pickle slices. Sprinkle with salt and pepper and top with remaining bread slices, mayonnaise side down.

Heat a large frying pan over medium heat. Add the sandwiches and weigh down with another heavy frying pan. Cook 2–3 minutes, or until bread is golden brown; flip over and cook the other sides until bread turns golden brown and cheese is melted. Alternately, cook the sandwiches in a panini grill until golden brown. Remove from pan and cut each sandwich in half. Makes 4 servings.

CLASSIC DAGWOOD SANDWICH

12	**thin slices white or wheat sandwich bread**
4 tablespoons	**mayonnaise,** divided
4 slices	**cheddar cheese**
4	**tomato slices**
$1/4$ pound	**thinly sliced ham**
8	**lettuce leaves,** divided
16	**dill pickle sandwich slices,** divided
2 teaspoons	**prepared mustard**
4 slices	**Swiss cheese**
$1/4$ pound	**thinly sliced cooked turkey**
4	**thin red onion slices**
2 tablespoons	**dill pickle relish**
8	**decorative toothpicks**

Spread 4 pieces of bread with half the mayonnaise and layer evenly with the cheddar cheese, tomato, ham, half the lettuce, and half the pickles. Spread 4 pieces of bread with mustard and top the sandwiches, mustard side down. Spread the other side of the bread with the remaining mayonnaise and layer evenly with the Swiss cheese, turkey, red onion, remaining lettuce, and remaining pickles. Spread the remaining 4 pieces bread with dill pickle relish and top the sandwiches, relish side down. Slice each sandwich diagonally with a sharp knife and skewer with a decorative toothpick. Makes 4 servings.

NEW ORLEANS PICKLE MUFFALETTA

1/2 cup	**chopped dill pickles**
1/4 cup	**chopped marinated artichoke hearts**
1/4 cup	**chopped pimiento-stuffed green olives**
1/4 cup	**chopped roasted red bell pepper**
1 can (2 ounces)	**sliced black olives,** drained
1	**large round loaf bread**
1/4 cup	**olive oil**
	salt and pepper, to taste
1/3 pound	**thinly sliced salami**
1/3 pound	**thinly sliced provolone cheese**
1	**small red onion,** cut into 1/4-inch slices
1/3 pound	**thinly sliced Swiss cheese**
1/3 pound	**thinly sliced ham**

In a small bowl, combine the pickles, artichoke hearts, green olives, bell pepper, and black olives. Cover and refrigerate for at least 2 hours, or overnight, to let the flavors develop.

Slice the bread in half around the middle and scoop out some of the soft bread in the center of loaf. Drizzle the olive oil on the inside of the top and bottom halves, and sprinkle with salt and pepper. Spread half of the pickle mixture on the bottom half of the bread. Alternate layers of salami, provolone, onion, Swiss cheese, and ham. Spread the top half of the bread with the remaining pickle mixture and press it down firmly on the top of the sandwich. Slice into 6 wedges. Makes 6 servings.

PICKLE AND TUNA MELT

¹/₃ cup	**mayonnaise**
2 tablespoons	**chopped dill or sweet pickles**
I tablespoon	**chopped onion**
I stalk	**celery,** finely chopped
I ¹/₂ teaspoons	**prepared mustard**
¹/₄ teaspoon	**Worcestershire sauce**
I can (6 ounces)	**tuna,** drained and flaked
	salt and pepper, to taste
2	**sandwich buns,** split and toasted
4 slices	**tomato**
4 heaping tablespoons	**grated cheddar cheese**

Preheat oven broiler and lightly grease a baking sheet.

In a small bowl, combine the mayonnaise, pickles, onion, celery, mustard, and Worcestershire sauce. Stir in the tuna and season with salt and pepper. Spread mixture over each bun half. Top each with a tomato slice and sprinkle with cheese, dividing evenly. Arrange on baking sheet and broil until cheese is melted. Makes 4 servings.

ZESTY REUBENS

2 tablespoons	**butter or margarine,** softened
8 slices	**rye bread**
1/3 cup	**Thousand Island Salad Dressing** (see recipe on page 22)
1/4 pound	**sliced Swiss cheese**
1/2 pound	**thinly sliced corned beef**
12	**dill pickle sandwich slices**

Butter one side of 4 bread slices and place butter side down in a cold frying pan. Spread each slice with the dressing, dividing evenly. Divide the cheese and arrange it on top of the bread, followed by the corned beef. Top each with 3 pickle slices. Add the remaining bread slices and spread the tops with butter. Heat the frying pan on medium and cook until sandwiches are lightly browned; flip and cook other side until browned. Cut on the diagonal and serve. Makes 4 sandwiches.

DILL PICKLICIOUS TURKEY WRAPS

4 (10-inch)	**whole wheat tortilla wraps**
4 tablespoons	**mayonnaise**
2 teaspoons	**prepared mustard**
1/3 pound	**sliced honey-roasted turkey**
8	**dill pickle sandwich slices**
4 slices	**dill Havarti cheese**
4	**Bibb lettuce leaves**
	salt and pepper, to taste

Warm each tortilla wrap on a plate in the microwave for 10 seconds. Combine the mayonnaise and mustard in a small dish and spread the mixture on each wrap, dividing evenly. Divide the turkey slices among the wraps and top each with 2 pickle slices, 1 slice cheese, and a lettuce leaf. Sprinkle with salt and pepper and roll each one up tightly. Cut on the diagonal and serve. Makes 4 wraps.

SCANDINAVIAN OPEN-FACE SANDWICH

3 tablespoons	**dill pickle relish**
2 teaspoons	**mustard**
4 slices	**rye bread**
12 slices	**Danish ham**
4 slices	**Jarlsberg cheese**
8	**baby dill pickles,** cut lengthwise into thin slices

Combine the relish and mustard and spread on each slice of bread, dividing evenly. Top each with 3 slices ham and 1 slice cheese. Arrange the pickles on top of each sandwich, fanning the slices. Makes 4 servings.

FRIED-PICKLE BURGERS

	vegetable oil
¹/₂ cup	**flour**
¹/₂ teaspoon	**baking powder**
¹/₂ teaspoon	**garlic powder**
I	**egg,** beaten
¹/₂ cup	**sliced dill pickles,** drained
¹/₄ teaspoon	**salt**
I pound	**ground beef,** shaped into 4 patties
4 slices	**American cheese**
4	**hamburger buns,** split and toasted
4 tablespoons	**ranch dressing**

Heat 2 inches of vegetable oil in a deep, heavy pan over medium heat to 370 degrees.

Combine flour, baking powder, and garlic powder in a shallow bowl. Pour the egg into a shallow dish. Dry the pickle slices on paper towels, dip pickles into the egg, and then into the flour mixture. Cook in the hot oil in batches, turning once, about 2 minutes, or until golden brown. Drain on paper towels, sprinkle with salt, and set aside.

Heat 2 teaspoons vegetable oil in a frying pan over medium heat and cook the ground beef patties, turning once, to desired doneness. Turn off heat, arrange I slice cheese on each patty, cover pan, and allow the cheese to melt.

Spread each bun top with I tablespoon ranch dressing. On bottom halves of buns, layer cheese-topped hamburgers, fried pickles, and bun tops. Makes 4 servings.

BRATWURST WITH PICKLES, BACON, AND ONIONS

6 slices	**bacon,** chopped
I cup	**chopped red onion**
I cup	**chopped dill pickles**
2 tablespoons	**apple cider vinegar**
I teaspoon	**sugar**
6	**bratwurst sausages**
$^1/_2$ cup	**water**
6	**French rolls,** split and toasted

Cook the bacon in a frying pan over medium heat for 5 minutes. Add the onion and cook until bacon is crisp and browned. Drain excess fat and add pickles, vinegar, and sugar. Cook for 3 minutes, stirring constantly. Cover and keep warm.

In a large nonstick frying pan, cook the bratwurst over medium-high heat until browned, about 5 minutes, turning links often. Reduce heat to medium-low. Add water to pan, cover, and simmer for 10–12 minutes, or until cooked through. Serve bratwurst on toasted rolls and spoon some of the relish on top. Makes 6 servings.

PICKLE AND HAM SALAD ROLLS

2 cups	**diced ham**
2 tablespoons	**chopped sweet pickle or sweet pickle relish**
2	**green onions,** chopped
$^1/_3$–$^1/_2$ cup	**mayonnaise**
1–2 teaspoons	**sweet pickle juice**
1	**stalk celery,** finely chopped
1	**hard-boiled egg,** peeled and diced
	salt and pepper, to taste
6	**lettuce leaves**
6	**soft hot dog rolls,** split, toasted, and buttered

In a food processor, combine the ham, pickle, and green onions. Pulse until minced; transfer to a medium bowl. Mix in enough mayonnaise and pickle juice to moisten mixture then stir in the celery and egg; season with salt and pepper. Arrange 1 lettuce leaf on each roll and spread with ham salad, dividing evenly among the rolls. Makes 6 servings.

PICKLE PIGS IN BLANKETS

I can (8 ounces)	**refrigerated crescent rolls**
6	**hot dogs**
6	**dill pickle sandwich slices**
3 slices	**Colby cheese**

Preheat oven to 350 degrees and lightly grease a baking sheet.

Unroll crescent rolls, pressing along diagonal perforations to seal, and shape into a single rectangle. Using a sharp knife, cut in half vertically and cut each half into 3 even pieces.

Make a cut down the center of each hot dog, about $2/3$ of the way through. Cut each pickle in half lengthwise and cut each Colby cheese slice into 4 pieces. Stuff 2 cheese strips and 2 pickle strips down the middle of each hot dog, overlapping cheese to fit. Arrange a hot dog vertically down the center of each piece of dough.

Wrap the dough around the hot dogs and pinch dough together to seal. Arrange on the baking sheet and bake for about 15–20 minutes, or until golden brown. Makes 6 servings.

PORK 'N' PICKLE BURGERS

I pound	**ground pork**
1/2 cup	**finely chopped ham**
I tablespoon	**dill pickle relish**
1/4 teaspoon	**salt**
1/4 teaspoon	**pepper**
1/3 cup	**chopped bread-and butter-pickles**
1/4 cup	**mayonnaise**
4	**sesame seed hamburger buns,** lightly toasted
4 thin slices	**sweet onion,** optional

Preheat a barbecue grill to medium heat and lightly grease the grill rack.

Combine the pork, ham, relish, salt, and pepper in a large bowl and mix well, using your hands to distribute the ingredients evenly. Shape into 4 patties and grill for several minutes per side to desired doneness.

Combine the pickles and mayonnaise in a small bowl. Arrange a pork burger on the bottom half of each bun, top with some of the pickle mixture, and a slice of onion, if desired, followed by the top bun. Makes 4 servings.

PICKLE SLIDERS

2 teaspoons	**vegetable oil**
1/4 cup	**chopped onion**
1 pound	**lean ground beef**
1/2 teaspoon	**salt**
1/4 teaspoon	**pepper**
4 slices	**American cheese**
1/4 cup	**mayonnaise**
2 tablespoons	**ketchup**
1/4 cup	**pickle relish**
12	**small rolls,** split and toasted
24	**dill pickle slices**

Heat the oil in a frying pan over medium heat and cook the onion until translucent, 3–4 minutes; cool to room temperature. Use a slotted spoon to transfer the onion to a medium bowl (do not wipe out the frying pan) and add the ground beef to the bowl. Mix thoroughly and turn the beef mixture out onto a work surface. Pat into a large rectangle, about 6 x 8 inches. Cut into 12 (2-inch) square patties and sprinkle with salt and pepper. Cut each cheese slice in half lengthwise and crosswise to make 4 small squares.

Reheat oil in the frying pan and cook the burgers over medium heat to desired doneness, about 4 minutes per side; top each with a cheese square. In a small bowl, combine the mayonnaise, ketchup, and pickle relish. Spread the sauce on the bottom half of the rolls. Top each roll with a hamburger patty, 2 pickle slices, and the roll tops. Makes 12 sliders.

GRILLED HAM, CHEESE, AND PICKLE SANDWICH

8 slices	**sourdough or white bread**
¼ cup	**mayonnaise**
1½ cups	**grated mozzarella cheese**
1½ cups	**grated Swiss cheese**
¾ cup	**bread-and-butter pickles**
12 slices	**deli ham**
6 tablespoons	**butter or margarine,** divided

Arrange 4 slices of bread on a work surface and spread with mayonnaise. Combine cheeses in a small bowl and sprinkle the bread slices evenly with half of the mixture. Layer each sandwich with half of the pickles, 3 slices ham, remaining pickles, and remaining cheese. Cover with remaining bread slices.

Melt 2 tablespoons butter in a large heavy frying pan over medium heat. Add 2 sandwiches to the pan and cook until bread is golden, about 4–5 minutes. Add 1 tablespoon butter to the frying pan, flip sandwiches, and cook until bread is golden and cheese is melted, about 3–4 minutes longer. Repeat process with remaining butter and sandwiches and cut each on the diagonal. Makes 4 servings.

STUFFED TURKEY BURGERS

1 1/4 pounds	**ground turkey**
1 teaspoon	**salt**
1/2 teaspoon	**pepper**
1/2 teaspoon	**cumin**
1/2 cup	**grated cheddar cheese**
1/3 cup	**finely chopped dill pickles**
1 tablespoon	**olive oil**
4	**hamburger buns,** split and toasted
4	**lettuce leaves**
4	**tomato slices**
8	**dill pickle slices**

In a large bowl, mix together turkey, salt, pepper, and cumin until combined. Divide mixture into 8 even-size balls. Put each ball between 2 pieces of waxed paper and use a rolling pin to flatten into a 4-inch circle. Transfer 4 patties to work surface and mound 2 tablespoons cheese in the center of each. Top each with a heaping tablespoon of pickles. Top with the remaining turkey patties, and use a fork to press and seal the edges.

Heat the oil in a frying pan over medium-high heat and cook the patties for 6–7 minutes on each side, until fully cooked and lightly browned. Serve on hamburger buns topped with lettuce, tomato, and pickles. Makes 4 servings.

BARBECUED PICKLE PORKWICHES

1 1/2 pounds	**boneless pork tenderloin**
	salt and pepper, to taste
1 tablespoon	**vegetable oil**
1 1/2 cups	**barbecue sauce**
2 tablespoons	**dill pickle juice**
6	**Kaiser rolls,** split and toasted
1/2 cup	**creamy coleslaw**
1/2 cup	**dill pickle slices**

Sprinkle the pork tenderloin with salt and pepper. Heat the oil in a large frying pan over medium-high and cook the tenderloin, turning several times, until browned, about 10 minutes. Drain on paper towels.

Combine the barbecue sauce and pickle juice in a 3-quart slow cooker and add the pork; cook on low for 6–8 hours, or until the meat is tender. Remove from the slow cooker, shred with a fork, and return to the cooker to coat with the sauce. Top each roll bottom with coleslaw, a generous serving of pork, pickle slices, and roll tops. Makes 6 servings.

SIDE DISHES & BREADS

ROAST PICKLE POTATOES

3 tablespoons	**dill pickle juice**
1 tablespoon	**olive oil**
1 tablespoon	**dried dill**
1 teaspoon	**garlic powder**
1 teaspoon	**paprika**
1 teaspoon	**salt**
3 pounds	**small, unpeeled new potatoes,** cut in wedges
3/4 cup	**dill pickle slices,** drained

Preheat oven to 350 degrees and lightly grease a baking sheet.

In a large bowl, whisk together the pickle juice, olive oil, dill, garlic powder, paprika, and salt. Add the potatoes and pickles and stir to combine. Spread mixture on the prepared baking sheet and bake, uncovered, until potatoes are tender, about 20 minutes. Makes 8 servings.

DILLY DEVILED EGGS

12	**hard-boiled eggs,** peeled
1/3 cup	**ranch salad dressing**
1/2 cup	**cream cheese,** softened
1/2 cup	**finely chopped dill pickles,** well drained
1/4 teaspoon	**salt**
	fresh dill sprigs, optional

Cut each egg in half lengthwise; gently scoop out yolks and place in a medium bowl. Mash yolks with a fork and stir in ranch dressing, cream cheese, pickles, and salt. Fill the hollowed egg halves generously with the egg yolk mixture. Chill in the refrigerator until ready to serve and garnish with fresh dill sprigs, if desired. Makes 24 eggs.

ZIPPY SUCCOTASH

1 tablespoon	**butter or margarine**
3–4 ears	**fresh corn kernels** (or 2 cups frozen corn kernels, thawed)
1 cup	**frozen lima beans,** thawed
1/2 cup	**chopped dill pickles**
1 jar (2 ounces)	**diced pimientos,** drained
1 teaspoon	**paprika**
1/2 teaspoon	**salt**
1/4 teaspoon	**freshly ground black pepper**
	chopped parsley for garnish

Melt the butter in a large frying pan over medium-high heat and cook the corn and lima beans, stirring occasionally, until tender, about 5 minutes. Add the pickles, pimientos, paprika, salt, and pepper and stir to combine. Continue cooking for 1–2 minutes, or until heated through. Garnish with parsley. Makes 6 servings.

SWEET AND SOUR VEGETABLES

3	**carrots,** peeled and cut into ¼-inch slices
½ pound	**green beans,** ends trimmed
I head	**cauliflower,** cut into florets
I tablespoon	**butter or margarine**
2	**small yellow squash or zucchini,** sliced
¾ cup	**chopped bread-and-butter pickle slices**
⅓ cup	**bread-and-butter pickle juice**
	salt and pepper, to taste

Bring a pot of lightly salted water to a boil over medium-high heat and cook the carrots, green beans and cauliflower until just tender, about 5 minutes. Drain and set aside.

Melt the butter in a frying pan over medium heat and cook the squash, stirring occasionally, until tender, about 6 minutes. Add the carrot mixture, pickle slices, and pickle juice and continue cooking, stirring occasionally, for 5 minutes. Season with salt and pepper. Remove from heat and let stand for 10 minutes, stirring occasionally, to allow flavors to meld. Makes 6 servings.

DILLY GREEN BEANS

6	**medium dill pickles**
I tablespoon	**olive oil**
I tablespoon	**balsamic or red wine vinegar**
I clove	**garlic,** peeled and minced
I teaspoon	**sugar**
1/4 teaspoon	**salt**
1/8 teaspoon	**dry mustard**
I pound	**green beans,** trimmed

Cut the pickles lengthwise into strips, about 1/4 inch wide; set aside. In a small bowl, whisk together the olive oil, vinegar, garlic, sugar, salt, and mustard to make dressing; set aside.

Bring a pot of lightly salted water to a boil, add green beans, and cook for 7–8 minutes, or until tender; drain thoroughly and pour the beans into a serving dish. Drizzle the dressing over the beans and stir several times to coat. Add the pickle strips and toss to evenly distribute.

Cover and let marinate at room temperature for 30 minutes, stirring occasionally to distribute dressing. Makes 8 servings.

DILL PICKLE BREAD

I cup	**dill pickle juice,** room temperature
I tablespoon	**instant active dry yeast**
I tablespoon	**sugar**
I tablespoon	**olive oil**
I tablespoon	**dried dill**
$1/4$ teaspoon	**salt**
I	**large dill pickle,** finely chopped
3 cups	**flour,** divided
I tablespoon	**cornmeal**

In a stand mixer or large bowl, stir together the pickle juice, yeast, and sugar. Add the olive oil, dill, salt, chopped pickle, and I cup of flour. Beat until incorporated. Gradually add the remaining flour, beating until the dough forms a soft, elastic ball and pulls away from the sides of the bowl.

Knead the dough on a floured work surface. Spray the inside of a large bowl with nonstick cooking spray, place the dough inside, and turn once to coat. Cover the bowl and leave in a warm place to rise until double in size, about I hour.

Turn the dough out onto a floured work surface and shape into a loaf. Spray a 9 x 5-inch loaf pan with nonstick cooking spray and dust with the cornmeal. Place the dough in the loaf pan and cover. Allow to rise in a warm place for about 40 minutes.

Preheat oven to 400 degrees. Use a sharp knife to make 3 diagonal slashes in the top of the dough and brush the top with water. Bake for 25–35 minutes, or until loaf is golden brown and makes a hollow sound when tapped. Remove from oven and cool in the pan for 5 minutes. Remove from pan and cool bread on a wire rack. Makes I loaf.

PICKLE BISCUITS

2 1/4 cups	**flour**
2 1/2 teaspoons	**baking powder**
2 teaspoons	**sugar**
3/4 teaspoon	**salt**
1/2 teaspoon	**baking soda**
1/2 cup	**cold butter or margarine,** cut into 1/2-inch cubes
1 cup	**grated sharp cheddar cheese**
1/3 cup	**finely chopped dill pickles,** well drained
1 cup	**buttermilk**

Preheat oven to 425 degrees and line a baking sheet with parchment paper.

In a medium bowl, whisk together the flour, baking powder, sugar, salt, and baking soda. Add the butter and use a pastry blender or 2 forks to blend mixture until it resembles coarse crumbs. Stir in the cheese and pickles. Add the buttermilk and stir just until the dough comes together. Do not over mix.

Turn out the dough onto a lightly floured work surface and pat it to a thickness of 3/4 inch. Cut rounds using a floured 2 1/2-inch biscuit cutter. Transfer to baking sheet and bake for 10–12 minutes, or until golden brown. Makes 12 biscuits.

CHEESY PICKLE AND ARTICHOKE MUFFINS

I can (16.3 ounces)	**jumbo refrigerated biscuits**
I tablespoon	**butter or margarine**
$^1/_4$ cup	**chopped onion**
$^1/_2$ cup	**chopped dill pickles,** drained
$^1/_2$ cup	**chopped cooked artichoke hearts**
$^1/_3$ cup	**sour cream**
$^1/_3$ cup	**cream cheese,** softened
I $^1/_2$ cups	**grated mild cheddar cheese,** divided
2	**eggs,** beaten

Preheat oven to 375 degrees. Lightly grease 8 cups of a 12-cup muffin tin. Evenly press the biscuits into the bottom and up the sides of the greased cups.

Heat the butter in a frying pan over medium heat and cook the onion, stirring, until translucent. Add the pickles and artichokes and cook for I minute. Remove from heat and cool for 5 minutes. In a large bowl, combine the pickle mixture, sour cream, cream cheese, I cup cheese, and eggs. Evenly spoon the mixture into prepared muffin cups. Bake 15 minutes. Remove from oven, sprinkle with remaining cheese, and continue baking for 5 more minutes, or until golden brown. Makes 8 muffins.

DINNERS

PICKLE CHEESEBURGER PIE

1 (8-inch)	**unbaked pie shell**
1 pound	**ground beef**
1	**small onion,** diced
2 cloves	**garlic,** minced
1/4 cup	**flour**
1/4 teaspoon	**salt**
2/3 cup	**dill pickle juice**
1/3 cup	**milk**
3/4 cup	**chopped dill pickles**
2 cups	**grated Colby cheese,** divided

Preheat oven to 425 degrees. Bake pie crust for 15 minutes and cool on a wire rack.

Crumble ground beef in a large frying pan and cook over medium heat for 2 minutes. Add the onion and garlic and continue cooking until beef is no longer pink. Drain grease and sprinkle with flour and salt. Stir in pickle juice and milk and stir until slightly thickened and bubbly. Add pickles and 1 cup cheese and stir just until combined. Spoon mixture into pie shell and sprinkle with remaining cheese. Bake for 15–20 minutes, or until pie shell is golden brown and cheese is bubbly. Remove from oven and let set for 5 minutes before serving. Makes 6 servings.

GRILLED PICKLE STEAKS

³/₄ cup	**olive oil**
³/₄ cup	**dill pickle juice**
¹/₃ cup	**sliced dill pickles**
I clove	**garlic,** peeled and minced
4 (¹/₂-pound)	**rib-eye steaks**
I teaspoon	**pepper**
¹/₂ teaspoon	**salt**
4 tablespoons	**Pickle Compound Butter**
	(see recipe on page 30)

Combine oil, pickle juice, pickles, and garlic in large shallow dish. Add steaks and turn until coated. Cover and marinate in refrigerator overnight, or up to 24 hours, turning steaks once or twice.

Preheat grill to medium high and lightly oil the grill grate. Grill steaks for 7 minutes per side, or to desired doneness, brushing with additional marinade during grilling. Discard remaining marinade and sprinkle steaks with pepper and salt. Top each steak with I tablespoon Pickle Compound Butter. Makes 4 servings.

DILL PICKLE MEATLOAF

³/₄ cup	**ketchup**
I	**egg,** lightly beaten
2 tablespoons	**Worcestershire sauce**
I tablespoon	**hot pepper sauce**
I	**large onion,** chopped
¹/₂ cup	**chopped dill pickles**
¹/₂ cup	**chopped fresh parsley**
¹/₂ cup	**breadcrumbs**
I ¹/₄ pounds	**ground beef**
³/₄ pound	**ground Italian sausage**
¹/₄ cup	**grated Parmesan cheese**

Preheat oven to 350 degrees and lightly grease a loaf pan.

In a large bowl, combine the ketchup, egg, Worcestershire sauce, and hot pepper sauce. Add the onion, pickles, parsley, and breadcrumbs; stir to combine. Add the ground beef and sausage and blend mixture with clean hands.

Press the mixture into the prepared loaf pan and bake for I hour, or until meatloaf reaches an internal temperature of 160 degrees. Remove from oven, sprinkle with cheese, and cook for 5 more minutes. Remove from oven and serve. Makes 6 servings.

CUBAN PORK TENDERLOIN

1 pound	**pork tenderloin,** trimmed
1 1/2 tablespoons	**olive oil**
1 clove	**garlic,** peeled and minced
1 teaspoon	**dried oregano**
2 tablespoons	**whole-grain mustard**
3 slices	**Swiss cheese,** halved
3 slices	**deli ham,** halved
1/3 cup	**chopped bread-and-butter pickles**
1/4 teaspoon	**salt**
1/4 teaspoon	**pepper**

Preheat grill to medium-high heat and lightly oil the grill grate. Cut a lengthwise slit down the center of the tenderloin 2/3 of the way through the meat. Open halves, laying tenderloin flat. Place tenderloin between 2 sheets of plastic wrap; pound to 1/2-inch thickness using a meat mallet or heavy frying pan.

In a small dish, combine the oil, garlic, and oregano. Rub the mixture on one side of the tenderloin. Turn it over and spread the mustard evenly over the other side. Arrange cheese slices evenly over the pork and top with the ham slices, layering evenly. Sprinkle the pickles evenly on top. Roll the pork loin starting from long side, and secure it at 1-inch intervals with kitchen string. Sprinkle evenly with salt and pepper.

Grill the pork for 20–25 minutes, turning several times during cooking, until a thermometer registers 160 degrees. Remove from grill to a cutting board, tent with aluminum foil, and let stand for 5 minutes before slicing. Makes 3–4 servings.

BBQ PICKLE PIZZA

I can (10 ounces)	**refrigerated pizza crust**
I cup	**barbecue sauce**
2 cups	**shredded, cooked chicken**
$1/2$ cup	**dill pickle slices,** drained
2 cups	**grated mozzarella cheese**
$3/4$ cup	**grated cheddar cheese**
I tablespoon	**butter or margarine,** melted
I clove	**garlic,** peeled and minced

Preheat oven to 425 degrees. Press pizza dough on lightly greased 12-inch pizza pan or baking sheet. Spread barbecue sauce evenly over dough; top with chicken, pickles, and both cheeses. Bake until crust is golden brown and cheese is bubbly, about 15 minutes.

While pizza is cooking, combine butter and garlic in a small dish and stir to combine. When pizza is done, remove pan from oven and immediately brush pizza crust edges generously with garlic butter. Transfer to a cutting board and cut into 8 slices. Makes 8 servings.

CREAMY DILL PICKLE CHICKEN

1/2 cup	**flour**
1/4 teaspoon, each	**salt and pepper**
8	**boneless, skinless chicken breasts**
2 tablespoons	**butter or margarine**
1	**medium onion,** chopped
1 cup	**chicken stock or broth**
2	**egg yolks**
1/2 cup	**coarsely chopped dill pickles**
1/4 cup	**dill pickle juice**
2	**green onions,** finely chopped
1 tablespoon	**chopped fresh dill weed** (or 1 teaspoon dried dill)
1/4 cup	**chopped fresh flat-leaf parsley**

In a shallow dish, combine the flour, salt, and pepper. Dredge the chicken in the flour mixture. Heat the butter in a large frying pan over medium-high heat. Add the chicken in batches and cook until browned and cooked through, 3–4 minutes per side. Transfer to a plate and tent with foil to keep warm.

Add the onion to the frying pan and cook over medium heat until lightly browned, about 5 minutes. Add the stock, increase heat to medium high, and bring to a simmer. Cook until slightly reduced, 3–4 minutes. Reduce the heat to medium low.

In a small bowl, combine the egg yolks, pickles, pickle juice, green onions, and dill. Ladle some of the hot stock into the mixture to temper the egg yolks and stir quickly. Stir the mixture back into the broth and cook, stirring, for 1–2 minutes, until sauce thickens slightly. Add the chicken to the frying pan and cook until the sauce thickens and the chicken is heated through, about 5 minutes. Serve garnished with chopped parsley. Makes 4 servings.

SALMON FILETS WITH DILL PICKLE SAUCE

4	**fresh salmon filets**
3 tablespoons	**butter or margarine**
3	**green onions,** chopped, including stems
I tablespoon	**finely chopped fresh dill weed** (or I teaspoon dried dill)
I tablespoon	**finely chopped parsley**
2	**large dill pickles,** diced
I tablespoon	**fresh lemon juice**
$^1/_4$ teaspoon	**salt**
$^1/_4$ teaspoon	**pepper**
$^1/_2$ cup	**seasoned breadcrumbs**

Preheat oven to 400 degrees. Place the salmon in an 8 x 8-inch glass baking dish.

In a small saucepan, melt the butter over medium heat. Add the green onions, dill, parsley, pickles, lemon juice, salt, and pepper and simmer gently for 5 minutes. Pour the sauce over the fish.

Cover the dish with foil and bake for 10 minutes. Remove the foil and sprinkle breadcrumbs over the salmon. Heat under the broiler for several minutes, until golden brown. Makes 4 servings.

BEEF PICKLE STROGANOFF

I tablespoon	**flour**
I cup	**beef broth**
I ¹/₂ tablespoons	**butter or margarine**
I tablespoon	**olive oil**
I	**medium onion,** thinly sliced
I ¹/₂ pounds	**beef tenderloin,** sliced into I x ¹/₄-inch strips
¹/₂ pound	**mushrooms,** sliced
¹/₂ cup	**sliced dill pickles**
2 teaspoons	**Dijon mustard**
I cup	**sour cream**
	salt and pepper, to taste
¹/₂ pound	**cooked egg noodles**
	finely chopped dill pickles

In a small bowl, combine the flour and broth and stir until blended; set aside.

In a large frying pan, heat the butter and oil over medium-high heat. When the mixture begins to sizzle, add the onion and cook, stirring, 4–5 minutes, until tender. Add the tenderloin and mushrooms and cook, stirring, 4–5 minutes, until tenderloin is cooked. Add the broth mixture and cook, stirring constantly, until mixture begins to bubble. Turn the heat to low, add the sliced pickles and mustard, and simmer for 2 minutes.

Remove the frying pan from the heat and stir in the sour cream. If sauce is too thick, thin with a little pickle juice or water. Season with salt and pepper. To serve, divide the noodles among 6 plates, top with the stroganoff, and garnish with chopped pickles. Makes 6 servings.

GERMAN ROULADEN ROLLS

1 1/2 pounds	**flank steak,** cut into 6 thin filets
2 tablespoons	**whole-grain mustard**
1/2 pound	**sliced Black Forest ham**
1	**large onion,** sliced
18	**dill pickle spears**
	salt and pepper, to taste
2 tablespoons	**butter or margarine**
2 1/2 cups	**beef broth**
4 tablespoons	**butter or margarine,** softened
4 tablespoons	**flour**

Spread one side of each filet with 1 teaspoon mustard. Lay the ham slices on the filets, dividing evenly. Sprinkle the onions on top. Arrange 3 pickle spears in middle of each filet. Sprinkle with salt and pepper. Roll the meat around the filling, securing the edges of each roll with several toothpicks.

Melt butter in a frying pan over medium heat. Add the rolls and cook, turning several times, until meat is browned. Add the broth and cook to simmering; reduce heat to medium low, cover and simmer for 1 hour, or until meat is tender.

Remove the rolls to a serving dish and tent with foil to keep warm. Combine the butter and flour in a small dish, mashing with a fork to form a smooth paste. Add the flour mixture to the pan juices in the frying pan and whisk to combine. Cook over medium-low heat, whisking constantly, until mixture thickens, 8–10 minutes. Adjust seasonings, if necessary. Serve the rolls with gravy spooned over top. Makes 6 servings.

MARINATED PICKLE CHICKEN

4	**whole chicken breasts**
I cup	**dill pickle juice**
2 tablespoons	**olive oil**
$1/4$ teaspoon	**salt**
$1/4$ teaspoon	**pepper**
4	**mini dill pickles,** sliced

Place the chicken breasts and pickle juice in a ziplock bag and refrigerate for 8 hours, or overnight.

Preheat the oven to 350 degrees. Heat the oil in a cast iron frying pan over medium-high heat. Remove the chicken from the juice and discard juice. Sprinkle the chicken with salt and pepper and add to the pan, skin side down. Cook for about 5 minutes, or until skin is golden brown. Flip over with tongs and continue cooking for 5 minutes.

Transfer the frying pan to the oven and bake the chicken for 50–60 minutes, or until the internal temperature reaches 160 degrees. Garnish chicken with pickle slices and serve. Makes 4 servings.

SLOW COOKER PICKLE PORK

1 jar (16 ounces)	**dill pickle slices**
1	**small onion,** sliced
1 (3½–4-pound)	**pork shoulder**
½ cup	**water**
2 cloves	**garlic,** peeled and minced
2	**shallots,** peeled and minced
	salt and pepper, to taste
8	**hamburger buns,** toasted
	coleslaw, optional

Drain the pickles and reserve ½ cup of the juice. Place half of the onion slices in the bottom of a 5 or 6-quart slow cooker. Remove and discard the outer skin and most of the fat from the pork shoulder. Place it on top of the onion, and add the water and reserved pickle juice. Top with the remaining onion, pickle slices, garlic, and shallots. Cover and cook on low for 6–8 hours, or until the meat is tender and shreds easily with a fork. Remove the pork shoulder and cool. Shred meat, season with salt and pepper, and serve with toasted buns and coleslaw, if desired. Makes 10–12 servings.

HAM AND CHEESE PICKLE POCKETS

I can (8 ounces)	**refrigerated crescent rolls**
4 teaspoons	**prepared mustard**
1/2 pound	**thinly sliced deli ham**
16	**dill pickle slices**
1/4 pound	**thinly sliced Swiss cheese**
2 tablespoons	**butter or margarine,** melted

Preheat oven to 350 degrees and lightly grease a baking sheet.

Unroll crescent rolls and separate dough into 4 rectangles, pressing along the diagonal perforations to seal. Spread each rectangle with I teaspoon mustard. Equally divide the ham slices and arrange on the bottom half of each rectangle; top each with 4 pickle slices. Equally divide the cheese slices and arrange over the pickles. Fold the dough over the filling ingredients to form a square. Press around the edges to seal and crimp edges with a fork. Brush each pocket with butter. Transfer to the prepared baking sheet and bake for 20 minutes, or until golden brown. Makes 4 servings.

SAUSAGE CALZONES

1 pound	**ground Italian sausage**
1	**onion,** thinly sliced
2 cups	**ricotta cheese**
1/2 cup	**chopped garlic pickles**
2 tablespoons	**chopped flat-leaf parsley**
2 cloves	**garlic,** peeled and minced
1/4 cup	**grated Parmesan cheese**
1/4 teaspoon	**pepper**
2 tablespoons	**chopped pimiento**
2 cans (10 ounces)	**refrigerated pizza dough**
2 cups	**grated mozzarella,** divided
1/4 teaspoon	**garlic powder**
2 tablespoons	**butter or margarine,** melted
2 cups	**marinara or spaghetti sauce**

Preheat oven to 425 degrees and lightly grease a baking sheet. In a large frying pan, brown the sausage over medium heat. Use a slotted spoon to transfer the cooked sausage onto paper towels to drain; crumble when cool. Discard all but 1 tablespoon of the drippings from the pan. Add the onions and cook on medium low, stirring occasionally, until golden brown.

In a large bowl, combine the sausage, onion, ricotta, pickles, parsley, garlic, Parmesan cheese, pepper, and pimiento. Unroll each pizza dough and cut in half crosswise. Spoon 1/4 of the filling on the bottom half of each of the 4 rectangles and top each with 1/2 cup mozzarella cheese. Fold dough over and pinch edges tightly to seal.

Transfer to prepared baking sheet. Combine garlic powder and butter and brush each calzone with the mixture. Bake for 15 minutes, or until golden brown. While the calzones are baking, warm the marinara sauce in a saucepan over medium heat. Remove calzones from oven and cool for 5 minutes. Serve with marinara sauce for dipping. Makes 4 servings.

PICKLE FONDUE

1 block (1-pound)	**Swiss or Monterey Jack cheese**
2 tablespoons	**flour**
1 cup	**milk**
1 clove	**garlic,** peeled and smashed
1 jar (16 ounces)	**baby dill pickles,** drained and dried on paper towels
1 loaf	**French baguette,** cut into 1-inch cubes

Grate the cheese into a medium bowl (do not use pregrated cheese). Add the flour and toss together with a fork until the flour coats the cheese.

In a saucepan or fondue pot, heat the milk and the garlic over medium-low heat until simmering, 2–3 minutes. Whisk the cheese mixture into the milk, a handful at a time, waiting until each handful melts before adding more. Whisk until cheese is completely melted and mixture is smooth and velvety.

To serve, keep the pot warm and use fondue forks to dip the pickles and bread cubes in the pot, swirling to coat with the cheese. Makes 4–6 servings.

FARMER'S CASSEROLE

2 pounds	**potatoes,** peeled and cut in 1/4-inch slices
2 cups	**diced cooked ham**
3 tablespoons	**butter or margarine**
2 tablespoons	**flour**
1 1/2 cups	**milk**
1/4 cup	**half-and-half**
1 cup	**grated cheddar cheese**
1/2 cup	**chopped dill pickles**
	salt and pepper, to taste

Preheat oven to 350 degrees and lightly grease a 2-quart baking dish.

Fill a large saucepan with water and bring to a boil over medium-high heat. Add the potatoes and cook for 10–15 minutes or until just tender; drain and cool.

Alternate layers of potatoes and ham in the prepared baking dish. Melt the butter in a large saucepan over medium heat and whisk in the flour. Gradually add milk and half-and-half and cook, stirring constantly, until sauce starts to boil. Add cheese and pickles and stir until cheese melts. Season with salt and pepper and pour sauce over potato and ham mixture. Bake for 30 minutes, or until lightly browned and bubbling. Makes 6 servings.

CHESAPEAKE CASSEROLE

I pound	**lump crabmeat,** picked through for shells
I cup	**cooked corn**
1/2 cup	**chopped dill pickles**
1/2 cup	**finely diced onion**
1/2 cup	**finely diced red bell pepper**
1/2 cup	**finely diced celery**
I cup	**light mayonnaise**
1/2 teaspoon	**dry mustard**
1/2 teaspoon	**red pepper sauce**
1/2 teaspoon	**seafood seasoning** (Old Bay)
1/2 teaspoon	**salt**
1/2 teaspoon	**pepper**
I	**egg,** slightly beaten
I 1/4 cups	**saltine cracker crumbs,** divided
1/2 cup	**Homemade Tartar Sauce** (see recipe on page 21)

Preheat oven to 325 degrees and lightly grease a 2-quart baking dish.

In a medium bowl, combine the crab, corn, pickles, onion, bell pepper, and celery and stir gently. In another bowl, combine the mayonnaise, mustard, pepper sauce, seafood seasoning, salt, and pepper. Stir into the crabmeat mixture and gently fold in the egg and I cup cracker crumbs. Spoon mixture into baking dish and sprinkle remaining cracker crumbs evenly over top.

Bake for I hour, or until bubbling and completely cooked through. Serve with Homemade Tartar Sauce. Makes 4 servings.

DESSERTS

PICKLE CUPCAKES WITH LEMON-CREAM CHEESE FROSTING

For the cupcakes:

6 tablespoons	**butter or margarine,** room temperature
$^1/_3$ cup	**sugar**
1	**egg**
$^1/_3$ cup	**sour cream**
1 cup	**flour**
$^3/_4$ teaspoon	**baking powder**
$^1/_4$ teaspoon	**baking soda**
$^1/_4$ teaspoon	**salt**
$^1/_3$ cup	**sweet pickle juice**
$^1/_3$ cup	**finely chopped sweet pickles**

For the frosting:

8 ounces	**cream cheese,** room temperature
$^1/_4$ cup	**butter or margarine,** softened
2 tablespoons	**lemon juice**
2 teaspoons	**lemon zest**
1 teaspoon	**vanilla extract**
5 cups	**powdered sugar**

Preheat oven to 350 degrees and line a 12-cup muffin tin with paper liners.

Beat the butter and the sugar in a large bowl until light and fluffy. Beat in egg and sour cream until blended. In a separate bowl, whisk together flour, baking powder, baking soda, and salt.

Alternate folding the flour mixture and pickle juice into the butter mixture in several batches until combined. Gently fold in the chopped pickles. Fill cupcake liners 3/4 full. Bake for about 25 minutes, or until a toothpick comes out of the cupcake clean. Cool to room temperature on a wire rack.

To make the frosting, beat the cream cheese, butter, lemon juice, lemon zest, and vanilla in a large bowl until smooth and fluffy. Add the powdered sugar, 1 cup at a time, beating after each addition, until creamy. If frosting is too thin, add more powdered sugar; if too thick, add a little pickle juice. Spread the frosting on the cooled cupcakes. Makes 12 cupcakes.

SWEET PICKLE ICE CREAM

2 cups	**heavy cream**
I cup	**whole milk**
³/₄ cup	**sugar**
4	**large egg yolks**
¹/₄ teaspoon	**salt**
3 tablespoons	**finely chopped sweet pickle,** well drained
I tablespoon	**sweet pickle juice**
¹/₂ teaspoon	**lemon extract**
	several drops green food coloring

In a medium saucepan, combine the cream, milk, sugar, egg yolks, and salt. Whisk to blend and cook over medium-low heat, whisking constantly, until mixture is thick enough to coat the back of a spoon, about 10 minutes. Pour mixture through a fine mesh strainer into a mixing bowl. Add pickles, pickle juice, lemon extract, and food coloring and stir to blend. Cover and chill for 2–24 hours.

Freeze the chilled mixture in an ice cream machine according to manufacturer's instructions. Transfer to a bowl, cover tightly, and freeze until firm. Makes 6 servings.

SWEET PICKLE PIE

2 cups	**sugar**
1 1/2 tablespoons	**cornstarch**
1 teaspoon	**cinnamon**
1 teaspoon	**nutmeg**
4	**eggs**
1 1/3 cups	**sweet pickle relish**
1 cup	**half-and-half**
2 tablespoons	**butter or margarine,** softened
1 teaspoon	**lemon extract**
1 (8-inch)	**unbaked pie shell**

Preheat oven to 350 degrees.

In a small bowl, combine the sugar, cornstarch, cinnamon, and nutmeg.

In a large bowl, combine the eggs, relish, half-and-half, butter, sugar mixture, and lemon extract; stir until well blended. Pour into pie shell and bake for 1 hour. Check the pie after 40 minutes. If crust starts to brown too much, cover the edges with foil or a pie crust ring for the last 20 minutes of baking. Cool on a wire rack. Makes 8 servings.

BIG DADDY PICKLE CAKE

2 boxes	**vanilla cake mix**
	green paste food coloring
3 sticks	**unsalted butter or**
	margarine, softened
1 ½ pound	**powdered sugar**
⅓ cup	**heavy cream**
3 tablespoons	**sweet pickle juice**
½ teaspoon	**vanilla**
pinch of	**salt**

Prepare each of the cake mixes according to package directions, adding ¼ teaspoon green paste food coloring to each batch of batter and baking each layer in a 9 x 13-inch pan. Cool the cakes on wire racks to room temperature, cover with plastic wrap and refrigerate for at least 2 hours, until firm.

On a piece of 9 x 13-inch light cardboard, draw a free-form pickle shape and cut out. Lay the stencil on top of each cake and use a sharp knife to cut the shape from the cake; reserve cake scraps for another use.

In a stand mixer fitted with the whisk, beat the butter at medium-high speed until creamy. Beat in the powdered sugar at low speed. Add the cream, pickle juice, vanilla, and salt and beat at medium-high speed until fluffy, about 3 minutes. If frosting is too thin, add more powdered sugar; if too thick, add a little more pickle juice. Stir in paste food coloring until frosting reaches desired shade of green.

Arrange 1 cake on a large serving platter and spread top with 1 cup frosting. Top with the second cake layer and evenly frost the top and sides. Put the remaining frosting in a decorator bag with a plain tip and make small bumps on the surface of the cake, if desired. Makes 24 servings.

NOTES

NOTES

METRIC CONVERSION CHART

Volume Measurements		Weight Measurements		Temperature Conversion	
U.S.	Metric	U.S.	Metric	Fahrenheit	Celsius
1 teaspoon	5 ml	1/2 ounce	15 g	250	120
1 tablespoon	15 ml	1 ounce	30 g	300	150
1/4 cup	60 ml	3 ounces	90 g	325	160
1/3 cup	75 ml	4 ounces	115 g	350	180
1/2 cup	125 ml	8 ounces	225 g	375	190
2/3 cup	150 ml	12 ounces	350 g	400	200
3/4 cup	175 ml	1 pound	450 g	425	220
1 cup	250 ml	2 1/4 pounds	1 kg	450	230

Check out these "101" favorites
for more tasty recipes:

Bacon	**More Ramen**
Beans	**More Slow Cooker**
Beer	**Pumpkin**
Bundt® Pan	**Ramen Noodles**
Cake Mix	**Rice**
Canned Biscuits	**Sheet Pan**
Casserole	**Slow Cooker**
Chile Peppers	**Toaster Oven**
Dutch Oven	**Tofu**
Grits	**Tortilla**
Instant Pot	**Tots**
More Bacon	

Each 128 pages, $9.99

Available at bookstores or
directly from GIBBS SMITH
1.800.835.4993
www.gibbs-smith.com

ABOUT THE AUTHOR

Eliza Cross is an award-winning writer, and the author of seven books. She develops recipes and styles cuisine for corporate and print media, and blogs about food, gardening, and sustainable living at Happy Simple Living. She lives with her family in Centennial, Colorado.